Eighteenth Century
—Encounters—

PREFACE

The chapters which follow are linked by four principal elements.
Each is concerned with England in a decisive phase of history,
that is the years surrounding the Hanoverian accession. They
mainly deal with the very earliest portion of the Georgian era,
namely the short but nevertheless momentous reign of George I.
Secondly, the studies are intended as explorations of the
commerce between life and art. Their point of departure is
located in significant historical events and movements: the
coming of the Hanoverian dynasty, the Jacobite scares, the
South Sea Bubble, the rise of Walpole, the beginnings of
organised crime. This is the age of the 'projector', that is to say of
ambitious entrepreneurs who undertook bold innovatory
ventures in trade, science and ideas. However, it is the artistic
response of major writers which occupies the centre of attention;
and in this lies the third common factor. Each chapter considers
the work of Defoe, Swift, Pope or Gay, by general consent the
greatest English authors active throughout the period. At the
heart of these matters stand a number of masterpieces composed
in the 1720s: *A Journal of the Plague Year, A Tour through the Whole
Island of Great Britain, Gulliver's Travels, The Dunciad* and *The
Beggar's Opera*—works which recur in the text of this book.
Finally, the studies are all meant to be elucidatory, rather than
exercises in critical method. In other words, they are designed not
to justify a particular mode of analysis, or to support a particular
ideology, but to reach into some of the contradictions and
complexities of a fascinating age by means of a close reading of
major works of literature, together with a careful scrutiny of
surrounding events.

In my view the great works of this period are dense with
historical resonance, and if we can make the leap from merely

noting inert topical 'references' to detecting more inward motifs (themes, organising principles, image-patterns and so on), we are much better placed to enjoy these enduringly powerful imaginative statements. Otherwise it is as though we should try to follow the tonal argument of a classical symphony without knowing its home key. The book is thus intended to provide a better acoustic for early Hanoverian England.

Historical information can all too easily become a distracting 'noise' which impairs our reception of the messages relayed by a past era. I hope *Eighteenth-Century Encounters* may help some readers to pick up more clearly what some great writers had, and have, to say. Hamlet remarks of Osric that he had 'only got the tune of the time, and the outward habit of encounter': to get the tune of a time as distant as that of the first Hanoverians now asks of us an active effort, whilst the 'habit of encounter' (which might be roughly paraphrased as 'outward manners') deters some readers from that effort. The word *encounters* in my title reflects a busy, combative strain in the culture of the day, when Swift could bandy words with the Queen Consort and Pope could engage in horseplay with a scandalous bookseller. The massive figure of Walpole enters the story at many points, and symbolises the public themes with which writers so energetically grappled. We might wish that our own encounters with Georgian life and thought should be equally lively, if a little less steeped in pain and danger.

P.R.

ACKNOWLEDGMENTS

Some portions of the book have appeared in a slightly different form as follows: Chapter 1 in *The Art of Jonathan Swift*, ed. Clive Probyn (Vision Press, 1978), 179-88; Chapter 2 in *Modern Language Review*, LXX (1975), 260-70; Chapter 4 in *Augustan Worlds*, ed. J. R. Watson *et al.* (Leicester University Press, 1978), pp. 107-118; Chapter 7 in *Papers on Language & Literature*, X (1974), 427-32; Chapter 9 in *Eighteenth-Century Studies*, VI (1973), 153-85. I am grateful for permission to reprint this material. In addition I am indebted to colleagues, students and friends who have afforded stimulus into argument and provocation into print.

ABBREVIATIONS

The following abbreviated forms are used in the notes to each chapter:

Carswell	John Carswell, *The South Sea Bubble* (London, 1960).
Defoe *Tour*	Daniel Defoe, *A Tour thro' the Whole Island of Great Britain*, ed. G.D.H. Cole (London, 1927).
LM Letters	*The Complete Letters of Lady Mary Wortley Montagu*, ed. Robert Halsband (Oxford, 1965–7).
Pope *Corr*	*The Correspondence of Alexander Pope*, ed. George Sherburn (Oxford, 1956).
Swift *Corr*	*The Correspondence of Jonathan Swift*, ed. Harold Williams (Oxford, 1963–5).
Swift *Poems*	*The Poems of Jonathan Swift*, ed. Harold Williams (Oxford, 2nd edn 1958).
Swift *Prose*	*The Prose Works of Jonathan Swift*, ed. Herbert Davis (Oxford, 1939–68).
TE	The Twickenham edition of Pope's *Poetical Works*, ed. John Butt *et al.* (London, 1938–67).

PRINCIPAL EVENTS 1714–28

1714	1 August	Death of Queen Anne: hastens collapse of Tory ministry.
	18 September	George I arrives in England.
	20 October	Coronation of George I.
1715	5 January	Parliament dissolved: general election (Whig victory).
	20 July	Riot Act passed.
	22 July	Habeas Corpus suspended.
	21 August	Death of Louis XIV.
	6 September	Earl of Mar raises the Pretender's standard.
	13 November	Battles at Sheriffmuir (inconclusive) and Preston (Jacobites defeated, and invasion halted).
	22 December	The Pretender lands at Peterhead.
1716	4 February	The Pretender departs from Montrose.
	24 February	Two of the rebel lords arrested.
	7 May	Septennial Act (to lengthen Parliaments) passed.
1717	January	Triple Alliance signed (England, France, Holland).
	31 March	Bishop Hoadly's sermon before the King sets off the Bangorian controversy.
	April	Whig split: Stanhope becomes first Lord of the Treasury, Townshend and Walpole ousted from ministry.
1718	August	Quadruple alliance (incorporating Austrian Empire).

1719	April-June	Abortive Jacobite expedition to Scotland.
	25 April	First part of *Robinson Crusoe* published.
	17 June	Death of Addison.
	8 December	Peerage Bill (limiting creations) rejected by House of Commons.
1720	12 May	Last two volumes of Pope's *Iliad* translation published.
	9 June	Bubble Act, outlawing companies without charter.
	late June	South Sea stock peaks at around 1000 (for £100 stock).
	September	Collapse of Bubble: stock falls to 180.
1721	4 February	Quarantine Act proclaimed (against plague).
	5 February	Death of Stanhope.
	3 April	Walpole succeeds Sunderland as first Lord and begins his long period of power.
1722	7 March	Parliament prorogued: general election: Whigs gain a further 38 seats.
	17 March	*Journal of a Plague Year* published.
	19 April	Death of Sunderland.
	16 June	Death of Marlborough.
	24 August	Atterbury arrested.
	9 October	New Parliament meets.
1723	25 February	Death of Wren.
	16 May	Atterbury arraigned before House of Lords and banished.
	May	Blacking episode at its height: Pope's in-laws implicated.
	22 May	Papists' Act passed (further restrictions on Catholics).
	27 May	Black Act passed.
1724		Wood's Halfpence affair.
	March-October	Swift publishes *Drapier's Letters.*
	21 May	First volume of Defoe's *Tour thro' Great Britain* published.

1725	24 May	Jonathan Wild executed.
	8 June	Defoe publishes *Life and Actions* of Wild and second volume of *Tour*.
	7 September	First volume of *The Complete English Tradesman* published.
1726	March–August	Swift visits England.
	9 August	Third volume of Defoe's *Tour*.
	28 October	Publication of *Gulliver's Travels*.
1727	20 March	Death of Newton.
	April–September	Swift's second visit to England.
	17 May	Second volume of *Complete English Tradesman* published.
	10 June	Death of George I.
	17 July	Parliament prorogued for general election.
	11 October	Coronation of George II and Caroline.

Addendum

1728	14 January	New Parliament meets: government majority now increased to 272, and Walpole strengthens his hold on power.
	29 January	First performance of *The Beggar's Opera*.
	14 February	Publication of *The Beggar's Opera*.
	14 May	First version of *The Dunciad* published.

FURTHER READING

The most up-to-date treatment of the years which occupy my attention in this book is to be found in Ragnhild Hatton, *George I: Elector and King* (London, 1978). Apart from primary texts by the leading authors, the following works can be recommended.

(*i*) A good general history is W.A. Speck, *Stability and Strife: England 1714–1760* (London, 1977). More specialised aspects of the political scene are treated in J.M. Beattie, *The English Court in the Reign of George I* (Cambridge, 1977); and A.J. Henderson, *London and the National Government 1721–1742* (Durham, N.C., 1945). On economic matters see J. Carswell, *The South Sea Bubble* (London, 1960); and P.G.M. Dickson, *The Financial Revolution: A Study in the Development of Public Credit 1688–1756* (London, 1967). There are interesting sidelights in Linda Colley, *In Defiance of Oligarchy: The Tory Party 1714–60* (Cambridge, 1982), especially Chapter 7.

(*ii*) Biographies are dominated by the two volumes of J.H. Plumb's life of *Sir Robert Walpole* (London, 1956–60), which straddle this period. Basil Williams, *Stanhope* (Oxford, 1932), remains informative, although chiefly on foreign affairs. G.V. Bennett, *The Tory Crisis in Church and State* (Oxford, 1975), is in effect a biography of Atterbury. For Jonathan Wild, see Gerald Howson, *Thief-Taker General* (London, 1970).

(*iii*) Wider cultural perspectives are explored by I. Kramnick, *Bolingbroke and his Circle* (Cambridge, Mass., 1968). Relevant to much of the present book is Peter Earle, *The World of Defoe* (London, 1976). Pope's political sympathies are provocatively assessed by E.P. Thompson in *Whigs and Hunters*

(Harmondsworth, rev. edn, 1977). See also H. Erskine-Hill, *The Social Milieu of Alexander Pope* (London, 1975). A new study is needed of the Pope/Curll quarrel: meanwhile, R. Straus, *The Unspeakable Curll* (London, 1927) contains solid fact amid facetious comment. Further discussion of all the writers who figure in this book will be found in my work *The Augustan Vision* (London, 1974): Swift and Pope also occupy a central place in *Hacks and Dunces* (London, 1980).

1
GULLIVER'S GLASSES

Lemeul Gulliver is perhaps the first bespectacled hero in English literature. Very early on we learn (I, ii) that he held back from the Lilliputians the contents of 'one private Pocket which escaped their search'.[1] These 'little Necessaries' were 'a Pair of Spectacles (which I sometimes use for the Weakness of mine Eyes) a Pocket Perspective, and several other little conveniences ... I apprehended they might be lost or spoiled if I ventured them out of my Possession'. From the start, then, Gulliver associates his glasses with secrecy, privacy, ownership, identity. I shall argue that this is connected with the mixed feelings about *sight* which Swift reveals, and that such a concern lies at the centre of the *Travels*. There will be three stages in the argument: a brief consideration of the psychology of spectacles; a discussion of attitudes to the faculty of vision in Swift's day; and then, at greater length, an application of these ideas to *Gulliver's Travels*.

I

Spectacles were not known to the ancients, which might suggest they would conveniently serve as a symbol for the moderns. (In *The Battel of the Books*, as a matter of fact, Descartes is killed by an arrow through his right eye owing to 'a *Defect* in his *Headpiece*'.)[2] Optical aids began seriously around the fourteenth century, but the major development came in the seventeenth. Charles I granted a charter to the guild of Spectacle Makers in 1629, and with the need for more accurate scientific lenses there was a steady improvement in the techniques of grinding glass—although Newton still had to cut his own prisms. By the eighteenth century portraits commonly show sitters equipped with reading glasses, perched on inquisitive or acquisitive faces. Benjamin Franklin invented bifocals around 1760 and claimed that he understood French better with the help of his spectacles—presumably for lipreading.

It is an elementary observation that spectacles flourished after the invention of printing, and indeed they have always been connected in people's minds with intellectual enquiry. They stand for a certain masterful negotiation of the external world. In popular writing they are often an emblem of vulnerability or retreat from the physical; the school swot is always duly equipped, whilst in Western movies the schoolma'am removes her glasses as she shakes down her hair in a well-understood gesture of sexual awakening. The presence of spectacles is often a clue to character in more serious literature, however: Mr Pickwick or Widmerpool would scarcely exist without this vital personal effect, and indeed we contemplate 'the bald head, and circular spectacles' of Pickwick before we learn anything at all about him—in the Phiz illustration they are the nearest thing to us in the entire scene, as Pickwick inclines forward at an angle. There is a feeling that someone who wears spectacles is not quite himself when bereft of them—yet a man who drops his glasses is comic, whereas a girl rooting about on the floor for a missing contact lens is merely embarrassing. (The glasses are separate from the self, whereas the contact lens is like an intimate part of the body itself.) Though they are intended to supply a defect of nature, spectacles can be *used*, as props in a lecture or as agents of a steely implacable gaze. They are allotted a special status, quite implausibly, as a mark of intelligence or curiosity. This is perhaps clearest with devices such as a lorgnette or quizzing-glass; it is interesting to note that (many productions of Restoration comedy notwithstanding) the quizzing-glass did not come in until about 1800, and in fact the word *quiz* with its associations of close interrogation dates from the same period. *OED* gives no usage earlier than the 1780s and reports a story that the word was invented by an Irish theatre manager as late as 1791. Whatever Lady Wishfort and her kind did, it cannot have been quizzing.

II

Poor eyesight abounded in Swift's day, and no-one can have been unaware of visual defects. There were many inherited conditions, with glaucoma sadly in evidence; total blindness must have been very much more common than today, although there are of course no firm statistics. Reading in semi-darkness cannot have improved things in a number of cases, and the obstinate Augustan determination to hold everything by candle-light, from funerals to auctions, seems like a perverse reinforcement. In 1710—the very year when Defoe left his glasses in Newcastle[3]— one of Swift's missions in London was to obtain two pairs of spectacles for Mrs Dingley: later he had to get a pair for Stella herself. A cargo sent back to Dublin finally included 'four pairs of spectacles for the Lord knows who'.[4] The *Journal to Stella* also records Swift's concern with the failing sight of his friend Congreve, by now almost blind with cataracts on both eyes. He mentions that Congreve can no longer read without magnifying-glass.[5] One recalls that by the age of forty Pope was unable to read by candle-light; though he enjoyed the friendship of the great surgeon William Cheselden, his last years were badly affected by eye troubles. Various afflictions beset Dr. Johnson, Burke and Horace Walpole (who acquired a pair of green glasses); Lady Mary Wortley Montagu at sixty-one was surprised enough to thank God that her sight served her yet without glasses.[6] Then there are the cases of musicians such as Bach, Handel and the blind composer John Stanley; Handel went more than once to Cheltenham and Bath to assist in his treatment, and it is not generally recognised that the valetudinarians at any spa included a large proportion of people with eye trouble. Of course, ophthalmic science was not very advanced; the princely Duke of Chandos asked his wine merchant amongst others for advice and was recommened to put Portuguese snuff in the corner of his eye. The merchant supplied a recipe involving first washing the eye in urine and then anointing it with viper's fat. Chandos got a second opinion from his doctor, who suggested confining the regimen to the viper's fat.[7]

Swift himself was subject to eye disorder. In the birthday poem he wrote for Stella in 1725 we get one of the few direct admissions:

Tis true, but let it not be known,
My eyes are somewhat dimmish grown;
For Nature, always in the Right,
To your Decays adapts my Sight,
And Wrinkles undistinguish'd pass,
For I'm asham'd to use a Glass;
And till I see them with these Eyes,
Whoever says you have them, lyes.

Characteristically, Swift's ostensible subject is the fact of *Stella's*
ageing. Sir Harold Williams comments, 'Even in old age Swift
refused to adopt spectacles'[8]. This may be put down to simple
vanity, but there seem to be deeper worries at hand. We have
heard a good deal about the progress of Ménières's disease, the
deafness and the giddiness; perhaps Swift felt just as acutely
about the loss of his visual powers, though he was less open about
the subject. It was generally agreed at this period that (in Locke's
words) sight was 'the most instructive of the senses'. As well as
Newton's *Opticks*, writers like Molyneux and Swift's friend
George Berkeley had erected a whole psychology of perception
around the faculty of vision. The importance for Swift of
developments in the microscope has been shown before now; it is
interesting to see him in a lighter mood, idling away the moments
until Harley falls in the summer of 1714, professing detachment
in the not-very-remote vicarage at Letcombe, as reported by
Pope in a letter to Dr. Arbuthnot:

> As for the methods of passing his time, I must tell you one which con-
> stantly employs an hour about noone. He has in his window an
> Orbicular Glass, which by Contraction of the Solar Beams into a
> proper Focus, doth burn, singe, or speckle white, or printed Paper, in
> curious little Holes, or various figures.[9]

Could a man with such a hobby speak innocently of the 'Glass' of
satire?

III

Meanwhile, back in Lilliput, Gulliver is hanging on to his optical
aids. He is, we notice, prepared to give up to his captors his

money, his watch, his guns, his razor, his handkerchief, his knife and even his 'Journal Book'. Contrast with this the reactions of Robinson Crusoe on his arrival at the island. When Crusoe lands, he has neither clothes nor weapon on his person: 'I had nothing about me but a Knife, a Tobacco-pipe, and a little Tobacco in a Box.' However, he makes twelve trips to the wrecked boat, bringing back a variety of stores and provisions. Among these things, though 'of less Value', he lists 'three or four Compasses, some Mathematical Instruments, Dials, Perspectives, Charts, and Books of Navigation, all which I huddel'd together, whether I might want them or no'. In point of fact it is nearly eighteen years before he apparently thinks to make use of his telescope, and takes a resolve 'to go no more out without a Prospective Glass in my Pocket'.[10] Crusoe has been too busy doing, making , creating. His daily life is organised around the objects he can see with the naked eye. There is no occasion for prying into the centre of things, for looking below the surface. Gulliver's trouble is that he is always trying to peer and peep.

One of the very few critics to have taken any account of Gulliver's spectacles, W.B. Carnochan, reaches the conclusion that he is 'the myopic hero' whose lack of understanding is symbolised by the weakness and vulnerability of his eyesight.[11] I think almost the opposite—that the glasses represent visual over-development, hypertrophy of the sight. Guliver lives through his gaze and his traveller's *curiosity* rather than through any settled principles or inner resources. His spectacles are, so to speak, bionic eyes, probing everywhere, hoarded lovingly like sexual attributes, secret, self-directed, protective. His 'insatiable Desire to see the World' is fed by his bespectacled competence as an observer. A common mistake, in my view, is to suppose that the narrator of the *Travels* is a mere victim of circumstance: a neutral patient rather than a constructive agent of his own fate. It is true that he is a man without qualities; but that is precisely the point. He has travelled so much, studied and applied himself—he measures everything down to the Brobdingnagian hailstones that fall on him—he is always *computing* (a favourite verb)—yet he has very little moral identity. He has been too preoccupied by watching to receive any direct impress from life. His character is an extension of that of Addison's *Spectator*—whose social background is closely allied, too.

Thus I live in the World, rather as a Spectator of Mankind, than as one of the Species: by which means I have made my self a Speculative Statesman, Soldier, Merchant and Artizan, without ever medling with any Practical Part in Life. I am very well versed in the Theory of an Husband, or a Father, and can discern the Errors in the Economy, Business and Diversion of others, better than those who are engaged in them; as Standers-by discover Blots, which are apt to escape those who are in the Game. I never espoused any Party with Violence, and am resolved to observe an exact Neutrality between the Whigs and Tories, unless I shall be forc'd to declare my self the Hostilities of either Side. In short, I have acted in all Parts of my Life as a Looker-on, which is the Character I intend to preserve in this paper.[12]

Ironically, it was a character not very remote from this self-dramatisation which Pope was to build into the portrait of Atticus. In each case 'neutrality' becomes a matter of withdrawal.

Now Gulliver's typical mode of withdrawal is through retreat into observation. The word *observe* and its derivatives occur some 140 times in the work: the frequency increases steadily from twenty-five in the first voyage, thirty-four in the second, thirty-eight in the third, to forty-five in the fourth. And, as in *The Dunciad*, the most horrific features of the satirist's world are beheld as a staged spectacle:

> All these, and more, the cloud-compelling Queen
> Beholds thro' fogs, that magnify the scene.[13]

Observation is generally delusive or futile. The Lilliputians who draw up an inventory of Gulliver's belongings, and mistake the purpose of all, speak of 'observing' (I, ii). The three great scholars ordered by the King of Brobdingnag to inspect Gulliver's person, likewise misleadingly, report in terms of observing, examining, viewing (II, iii). Gulliver himself, delightedly imagining the blessings of Struldbrugg existence, draws up a prospective list of 'Observations' and 'Discoveries' he would make if granted an extended term of life (III, x). *Discoveries* similarly carries malign overtones; it occurs in connection with gunpowder, when the King of Brobdingnag protests he would 'rather lose Half his Kingdom than be privy to such a Secret' (II, vii), and again where the Yahoos dig for the shining stones (IV, vii). Gulliver's role as looker-on, rather than participant, is emphasised at points where he witnesses events as a scene or tableau. He speaks of 'the whole Scene of this Voyage' (II, i); he dilates upon the 'Prospect' of Balnibarbi (III, iv), and indeed he climbs hills in order to gain a better prospect, like an eighteenth-century landscape painter. There is a fanciful or poetic quality to this viewing at times: the 'entertaining Prospect' of Lilliput strikes Gulliver thus:

> The Country round appeared like a continued Garden; and the inclosed Fields, which were generally Forty Foot square, resembled so many Beds of Flowers ... I viewed the Town on my left Hand, which looked like the painted Scene of a City in a Theatre.

Though he claims to be averse to such 'Spectacles', he visits an execution in Brobdingnag, and the spouting up of the blood reminds him of 'the great *Jet d'Eau* at *Versailles*' (II, v). He tells us he has 'often seen' the parade of the militia in Lorbrulgrud: 'Imagination can Figure nothing so Grand, so surprising and so astonishing. It looked as if ten thousand Flashes of Lightning were darting at the same time from every Quarter of the Sky' (II, vii). Small wonder that Swift recalled the book as a succession of graphic episodes and not as a bare allegory, a fact amply confirmed by his letter to Motte of 28 December 1727.[14] A favourite formula is 'I have seen ...', used of such prominent episodes as the rope-dancers (I, iii), or the Houyhnhnm mare threading a needle (IV, ix).

All this amounts to what might be called the drama of perception. The basic technique is to control the narrative through sense impressions; passages are introduced with verbs indicating Gulliver's awareness of what is happening to him. Thus in Lilliput, when he first awakes in his bound condition, we have *I found my Arms and Legs were strongly fastened/ I likewise felt several slender Ligatures across my Body/ I could only look upwards/ I heard a confused Noise/ I felt something alive/ I perceived it to be a human Creature/ I felt at least Forty more*—all within fifteen lines of print. Similarly the narrative of his being carried off by an eagle (II, viii) is shaped by the perceptual verbs: *found, felt, looked, could see, heard, began to perceive, observed, heard, felt, could see, perceived,* and so on. When he visits the Grand Academy of Lagado, virtually every paragraph begins with a brief introductory formula (*I*

saw/ I visited) which fix our attention on Gulliver as observer or
receiver (III, iv–v). An identical technique is found in the passage
describing the parade of ghosts at Glubbdubdrib (III, vii). It
would be natural to find some such usages, but their density goes
far beyond the functional requirement of keeping the sights
passing before us.

The most striking motif Swift employs is that of associating
vision and surprise, usually pained surprise. There are many
such episodes, with one or more characters (often but not
necessarily Gulliver) gawping in disbelief at some unexpected
sight. This happens when the Blefuscudians 'perceive' Gulliver
pulling the fleet and begin to scream in despair (I. v). Or when he
is taken home by the farmer in Brobdingnag, and shown to the
farmer's wife: she screams 'as Women in *England* do at the Sight
of a Toad or a Spider' (II, i). Or when Gulliver himself is
'confounded at the Sight of so many Pigmies', as are the sailors
who have rescued him (I, viii). Or when the first Yahoo and first
Houyhnhnm encounter Gulliver 'with manifest Tokens of
Wonder' (IV, i). Or when the Portuguese sailors gaze 'in
Admiration' at his strange appearance (IV, xi).[15] Sight has come
to express the ordeal of consciousness. Moral outrage is preceded
by some affront to visual expectation; contrary to the popular
view, most outbursts of negative feelings in *Gulliver's Travels* occur
when something nasty is *seen*, not smelt.

It is in this context that we should take account of the many
explicit references to the faculty of sight. I mean such events as
the arrow which narrowly misses Gulliver's left eye in Lilliput;
the use of his glasses as protection against the Blefuscan fusillades
(I, v); the plan to put out Gulliver's eyes, an 'Operation' which
might easily be interpreted as castration (but not by Gulliver,
who is less worried about sexual prowess than decency); the sight
of the nurse's breasts in Brobdingnag, where the defects are
apparent as though they have been viewed through a magnifying
glass (II, i); the old man with his eyes behind their spectacles 'like
the Full-Moon shining into a Chamber at two Windows' (II, ii);
the lice-ridden beggars, viewed again as through a
microscope—another sight/nausea connection (II, iv); the
problems of readjustment to the smallness of everything, after
Gulliver has returned from Brobdingnag (II, viii); the absurd
astronomers in Laputa, with their superior telescopes (III, iii);

Gulliver's horror at his own reflection in Houyhnhnmland (IV, x); or his ability to see a remote island through his pocket-glass, where the sorrel nag can distinguish nothing (IV, x). These episodes serve different rhetorical ends, but in each case seeing brings either pain or unwelcome news. It is as though looking too hard were an aggressive act for Swift, liable to shift into physical piercing of the object beheld. And in the passage at the close of Book II we have a dislocation of visual function used to point up a moral confusion.

IV

My argument has been this. Gulliver's quasi-objectivity as Spectator, the one who *observes*, represents the intrusive intellect; the over-intent scrutiny of what is better left unexamined, because it causes pain and revulsion when pried into by the modern empiricist. He basically wishes to peep, as from the back window of Don Pedro's house, but not be peeped at (as he is by the monkey during Glumdalclitch's absence). The glasses are the badge of his meddling and inquisitive nature. Thus far Gulliver is a satiric butt, standing for curiosity as against purposeful, spiritually directed living. But on another level Swift shares Gulliver's instincts, to hide and to peer out, to avoid bodily contact which squeezes and pains us. He wants to do this while at the same time negotiating at a safe distance with the physical world, through his sight. It is instructive that Swift has made Gulliver reliant for his very survival on spectacles, an aid which (as Swift admitted in his poem to Stella) he needed but was too proud to employ. The desire to transcend the body—that is, to ignore the inescapable limitations of human existence—was a proper object of satire for Swift. But the desire to escape from the body—to conceal its frailties and repress its urges—was Swift's very own, and its expression in *Gulliver's Travels* should call out our pity and not our scorn. We do not share Gulliver's pride but we are accomplices in his shame.[16]

Notes

1. Textual references follow Swift, *Prose*, vol. XI: page references are not given but the number of books and chapters is supplied. This paper is based on a lecture given under the Winston Churchill Foundation at the University of Bristol in 1976; I am grateful to some of those who heard it, now my colleagues, for useful criticism and comments.
2. *A Tale of a Tub*, ed. A. C. Guthkelch and D. Nichol Smith (Oxford, 1958), p. 244.
3. *The Letters of Daniel Defoe*, ed. G. H. Healey (Oxford, 1955), p. 305.
4. *Journal to Stella*, ed. Harold Williams (Oxford, 1948), I, 81, 88, 95, 97, 149; II, 389-90, 402.
5. *Journal to Stella*, I, 69, 305; II, 455. For Pope's relations with Cheselden, see M. H. Nicolson and G. S. Rousseau, *This Long Disease, My Life* (Princeton, 1968), pp. 58-61.
6. *LM Letters*, II, 474. Lady Mary is commenting on the case of the Duke of Montrose, who had gone blind before reaching the age of forty. I have of course omitted the names of many less important writers such as Dennis, Gildon, and Oldmixon, who suffered extremely severe ailments of the eye.
7. C. H. Collins Baker and Muriel I. Baker, *The Life and Circumstances of James Brydges First Duke of Chandos* (Oxford, 1949), p. 424.
8. Swift *Poems*, II, 757-8. A similar reluctance to wear glasses was exhibited by Mary Wollstonecraft and (for many years) Marcel Proust.
9. Pope, *Corr*, I, 234.
10. *Robinson Crusoe*, ed. J. Donald Crowley (Oxford, 1972), pp. 47, 64, 164.
11. W. B. Carnochan, *Lemuel Gulliver's Mirror for Man* (Berkeley and Los Angeles, 1968), p. 135. See also Denis Donoghue, *Jonathan Swift: A Critical Introduction* (Cambridge, 1969), pp. 59-85, on the optical 'perspectives' of satire.
12. *The Spectator*, ed D. F. Bond, 5 vols. (Oxford, 1965), I, 4-5.
13. *TE*, V, 275.
14. Swift, *Corr*, III, 257-58. I have discussed this letter in *The Augustan Vision* (London, 1974), pp. 195-96.
15. There are many other examples, including the reaction when Gulliver fires his pistol (I, ii); when he eats a sirloin bones and all (I, vi); when he arrives at the port of Blefuscu (I, viii); and when the Houyhnhnms conduct a general inspection (IV, iii). all these link sight and surprise: 'observation' is commonly in evidence.
16. For a strongly dissenting view, which takes up many of the issues raised in this chapter, see Carole Fabricout, *Swift's Landscape* (Baltimore, 1982), esp. pp. 186-96, 287.

2

GULLIVER AND THE ENGINEERS

> But there is another species of projectors, to whom I would willingly
> conciliate mankind; whose ends are generally laudable, and whose
> labours are innocent; who are searching out new powers of nature, or
> contriving new works of art; but who are yet persecuted with
> incessant obloquy, and whom the universal contempt with which
> they are treated often debars from that success which their industry
> would obtain, if it was permitted to act without opposition. Samuel
> Johnson, *Adventurer* no. 99, 1753.

On 13 February 1724 Jonathan Swift wrote to a friend of a letter
he had received from Viscount Bolingbroke, in which that lord
'raillyes [him] upon [his] Southern Journey'.[1] The allusion is to
Gulliver's Travels, then well towards completion. There are
disagreements about the exact chronology of the book's
composition. But it is generally accepted that ('whether or not
Gulliver's Travels embodies an older plan and older fragments, all
going back to the activities of the Scriblerus Club in 1714') the
actual writing was substantially performed between 1721 and
1725.[2] However, the allusion carries other overtones. No one
could write of a 'Southern' journey in the early 1720s without
calling up painful memories of the great Bubble. Few recent
events had bitten more deeply into the national psyche; and
though Swift was relatively insulated in Dublin, he wrote one
poem specifically on the subject and made repeated reference to
it in prose and verse.[3]

Equally, the text of the work itself suggests this strand of
allusion. At the start of the first book, Gulliver states that he
'accepted an advantageous Offer from Captain *William Prichard*,
Master of the *Antelope*, who was making a Voyage to the *South-
Sea*'. However, he remarks that 'it would not be proper ... to
trouble the Reader with the Particulars of our Adventures in

11

those Seas' (p. 20). In spite of this disclaimer, the voyage to
Lilliput remains a South-Sea 'adventure' of an unusual kind, a
fact of clear satiric charge in 1721. The voyage to
Houyhnhnmland likewise results from a commission to trade
with 'the *Indians* in the *South-Sea*' (p. 222). The phrase does not
occur directly in the other voyages, but both involve journeys to
southern waters—that to Brobdingnag, indeed, begins with 'a
Southern Wind, called the Southern *Monsoon*', raising up a storm
(p. 84). In strict usage the South Sea trade was that conducted
with South America and the islands of the Pacific. But in
ordinary speech any sailor who passed the Equator (in whichever
ocean) was travelling the South Seas. Swift's 'Southern Journey'
assuredly had that implication.[4]

But if the Bubble is thus invoked, it suggests that we should be
looking for even more topical meanings in the satire. Generally
critics have chosen to relate *Gulliver's Travels* to earlier
Scriblerian plans, to apply political satire to Swift's London
period, and to see the 'projects' of Lagado as chiefly parodies of
Royal Society experiments. I believe that these are mistaken
emphases. My sense of *Gulliver's Travels* is of a racy,
contemporary kind of satire, built up from immediate instances.
Overall it has much more to do with the world of Walpole and
Townshend than that of Harley or Godolphin. And the wild
schemes of Book III can be related to something far more direct
and close at hand than the elitist science of the 1690s. In fact, the
best location for sources and analogues, as far as projects go, is not
the *Philosophical Transactions* but the columns of newspapers in the
Bubble era and the patent applications of the day. *Gulliver's
Travels* was written at a time of exuberant commercial expansion
and fertile practical invention. Its cultural matrix can be defined
as the Age of Projectors—a bustling, uncerebral world of
entrepreneurs and inventors. Samuel Johnson was able to give
this a qualified welcome; but for Swift the search for 'new powers
of nature' merited the contempt and obloquy they attracted.
This stage in economic history was brought to a head in the
Bubble, itself a symbol of this speculative mania. Swift, I shall
argue, meant to site Lagado nearer Exchange Alley than
Gresham College.

I

In the fourth chapter of Book III, Gulliver meets the former governor of Lagado, Lord Munodi. He learns how, about forty years ago, 'certain Persons' paid a visit to the flying island of Laputa, and came back full of 'Schemes of puting all Arts, Sciences, Languages, and Mechanicks upon a new Foot. To this End they procured a Royal Patent for erecting an Academy of Projectors in *Lagado*.' In these newly established colleges, Munodi explains, 'the Professors contrive new Rules and Methods of Agriculture and Building, and new Instruments and Tools for all Trades and Manufactures, whereby, as they undertake, one Man shall do the Work of Ten'. Unfortunately, these 'Projects [were not] yet brought to Perfection', and so Munodi himself, 'being not of an enterprizing Spirit ... was content to go on in the old Forms' (pp. 176–7). The diction here ('Mechanicks', 'Patent', 'Projects', 'Trades and Manufactures', 'enterprizing') strongly suggests the world of commercial exploration. None of these terms are as appropriate to Royal Society ventures.

Munodi then gives Gulliver a concrete illustration:

> He only desired me to observe a ruined Building upon the Side of a Mountain about three Miles distant, of which he gave me this Account. That he had a very convenient Mill within Half a Mile of his House, turned by a Current from a large River, and sufficient for his own Family as well as a great Number of his Tenants. That, about seven Years ago, a Club of those Projectors came to him with Proposals to destroy this Mill, and build another on the Side of that Mountain, on the long Ridge whereof a long Canal must be cut for a Repository of Water, to be conveyed up by Pipes and Engines to supply the Mill: Because the Wind and Air upon a Height agitated the Water, and thereby made it fitter for Motion: And because the Water descending down a Declivity would turn the Mill with half the Current of a River whose Course is more upon a Level.

Munrodi reluctantly 'complyed with the Proposal', but 'after employing an Hundred Men for two Years, the Work miscarryed, the Projectors went off' to put others 'upon the same Experiment' (pp. 177–8).[5]

As regards the content of the satire here, it is worth considering the major changes in economic life in the previous forty years. In fact it was around the time of the Revolution that a great burst of projecting broke out, as Carswell describes:

> No age has been richer in [projectors], or more fertile in solutions to all human problems ... Between 1660 and the end of the century 236 patents were taken out—thirty-two more than in the succeeding forty years—and of these more than a quarter were granted in the three years 1691-3 ... In a successful project the patent was only the first story. The second was a joint stock company, and most of the joint stocks that leapt into existence in the wake of the Revolution were for the exploitation of patents.

It is likely that Swift has a subsidiary political point: undesirable innovations include the kind of notions imported when the English leaders went across to Holland to invite over William of Orange. But the main drift seems to be directed against the mania for commercial ventures based on credit and the City institutions. In fact Swift specifically linked the rise of public credit to the Revolution dynasts, notably Bishop Burnet, in his *History of the Four Last Years of the Queen*.

In this light we may glance ahead for a moment to the buildings of the Academy of Lagado. 'This Academy', says Gulliver, 'is not an entire single Building, but a Continuation of several Houses on both sides of a Street; which growing waste, was purchased and applyed to that Use' (p. 179). Arthur Case notes that this description does not fit the Royal Society's headquarters, and suggests that 'it is not impossible that [it] should be applied rather to the rapidly expanding governmental buildings on both sides of Whitehall'. However, though Whitehall was laid 'waste' after the fires of 1691 and 1698, no extensive purchases or reallocations of land were made; as Defoe reported in 1725, 'Many Projects have been set on foot for re-building the Antient Palace of *White-hall*; but most of them have related rather to a Fund for raising the Money, than a Model for the Building.' However, one major development of the period was the migration of stock-jobbers, after an act limiting their number in 1697, across the road from the Royal Exchange to Exchange Alley, whereupon 'the centre of business moved with them': 'The miniature labyrinth of lanes called Exchange Alley is still there, in the acute angle formed by Lombard Street and

Cornhill ... The whole maze, with its six entries (two in Lombard Street, two in Cornhill, and two in Birchin Lane) and two great trading coffee-houses, Garraway's and Jonathan's, covered an area rather smaller than a football pitch.'[6] In this case there was extensive rebuilding and some buying up of existing property; there was 'a Continuation of several Houses on both sides of a Street', rather than a straggling palace, and there was a phase of sudden growth in the 1690s. The Whitehall site was not restored after 1698 and, despite Defoe's hopes, never was in any substantive way.

But if this is the satiric drift here, the vehicle remains to be identified; it is a sustained allusion to engineering innovations of the period. Again we are reminded not of academic laboratory work but of actual developments in the application of mechanical science. For example, it was in the second decade of the eighteenth century that the famous Lombe silk mill was set up at Derby. In the third volume of his *Tour thro' Great Britain*, published just two months before *Gulliver's Travels*, Defoe noted 'a Curiosity in Trade worth reporting, as being the only one of its Kind in *England*':

> namely, a Throwing or Throwster's Mill, which performs by a Wheel turn'd by the Water; and though it cannot perform the Doubling Part of a Throwster's Work, which can only be done by a Handwheel, yet it turns the other Work, and performs the Labours of many Hands. Whether it answers the Expence or not, that is not my Business.
>
> This Work was erected by one *Soracole*, a Man expert in making Mill-Work, especially for raising Water to supply Towns for Family Use.

Defoe goes on to describe 'a very odd Experiment' Sorocold made here. Of course, it is not likely that Swift had this particular mill in mind. But it is precisely the kind of commercial innovation then in the news (John Lombe had gone to Italy to learn the secrets of silk-throwing machinery in 1716, and had taken out the first British patent in 1718). Moreover, the verbal echoes ('erected') and similarities of concept ('performs the Labours of many Hands') plainly indicate a common basis.[7]

George Sorocold was very much a man of his time. He was engaged from early in the century in devising lifting pumps and water-supply installations. He had worked on Tyneside and in

Scotland, and like many engineers had struggled with the then almost intractable problem of keeping coal-mines from flooding. Among those involved in this effort were the two most famous engineers of the age, Thomas Savery and Thomas Newcomen, pioneers of the steam engine. Before the turn of the century Savery, a military engineer, had applied to the House of Lords for the 'Encouragement of a new Invention . . . for raising Water, and occasioning Motion to all Sorts of Mill-Work by the impellent Force of Fire'. In 1702 the *Post Boy* carried a puff of true Laputan confidence regarding 'Captain Savery's Engines which raise Water by the Force of Fire in any reasonable quantities and to any height being now brought to perfection and ready for publick use'. Savery's pump was tried by the York Buildings Company (of whom more in due course), but proved a failure. A similar claim was made in an advertisement in the *London Gazette* on 14 August 1716, when the proprietors of the new engine set out their proposals from the Sword Blade coffee-house—a real Bubbler's address.

A still more celebrated figure in the history of technology is Thomas Newcomen, who at one time was in partnership with Savery. His machine followed Savery's at the York Buildings around 1726. He died in 1729 and by the early 1730s increasing financial difficulties caused the use of his pump to be discontinued by the Company. Both engines had come in for satire in papers such as Read's *Weekly Journal*, and any reasonably well-read contemporary (even in Dublin) would have been aware of what was afoot.[8]

The York Buildings Company by this time had a peculiarly bad reputation as an archetypal speculative enterprise. It had been set up to manage a waterworks near the Strand in London, but at the time of the Bubble opened a subscription of more than a million pounds in order to buy up forfeited estates. To make matters worse, its leading light from 1719 was a certain Case Billingsley, a solicitor, stockjobber, and company promoter, heavily involved in 'the murky legal battles' surrounding a marine insurance scheme. He was in fact a sort of successful Defoe, in business terms. By 1720 his interests included the Mines Royal, the Royal Lustring Company, and the Welsh mineral fields, which earn him in combination the right to be called the ultimate projector.[9] He was a moving spirit in the dubious

Harborough Lottery. In June 1724 he applied to patent a water-engine, as neat a tie-up as could be wished.[10]

Conveniently to our purposes, the surviving applications for patents, generally sent by the Secretary of State's office to the Attorney General for confirmation, afford many glimpses of projectors in action. One of the names to turn up most frequently is that of William Wood, hero of the *Drapier's Letters*, who was constantly fertile in schemes to exploit minerals or develop engineering techniques. Another regular applicant is Richard Newsham of London, in 1721 describing himself as a pearl-button maker, by 1725 styled an engineer. He devised a water-engine for extinguishing fires and another contrivance for raising water.[11] But the latter was something attempted by many. For example, in 1721 and 1722 John Orlebar, a Master in Chancery, was busy promoting his machine to 'deliver water to any height'—another scheme which got into the public prints. Several others were promoted around April 1724 and again in 1725 and 1726. August 1724 saw a 'wind engine or machine' for mill work.[12] One need not suppose that Swift knew or cared about many individual instances to conclude that he must have been aware of the trend—particularly as contemporary satires regularly linked water-pumps with fraudulent speculation. For example, *The Broken Stock-Jobber's Epilogue by a Loser* (1720) contains these lines:

> Why must my stupid Fancy e'er admire
> The way of raising up by Fire?
> That cursed Engine my Pockets dry,
> And left no Fire to warm my fingers by.

A better-known production, *The Bubbler's Mirrour, or England's Folly* (1721), has this: 'Some projects are all Wind, but ours is Water.'[13] Swift could hardly have referred to a 'project' for pumping water in the early 1720s without calling up, deliberately or not, such associations. In the light of Book III as a whole, it seems much more likely that the effect is a conscious one.

II

When we turn to the Academy of Lagado itself, in the fifth and sixth chapters, the idea of 'projects' remains powerful. In fact the terms 'project'/'projector' occur at least twelve times in the section on Lagado alone, together with 'engine', 'machine', 'inventor', and allied expressions. Gulliver even alludes to controversies over the right ownership of inventions, a matter which came to public attention chiefly through commercial claims and counter-claims.[14] Marjorie Nicolson and Nora Mohler are certainly correct to see in this section a satire on 'academicians in general and the Royal Society in particular'; but this is not a complete statement of the contents.[15] For example, the projector attempting to replace silkworms with spiders might recall the scheme for silkworms in Chelsea Park mentioned in the *Political State*'s list of peculiar and fraudulent enterprises during the Bubble year. The anal pump used on a dog, with fatal results, might be set alongside the 'air-pump for the brain' promoted at this time. Other schemes reported (real or fantastic) include one to extract butter from beech trees; one for insurance on horses; one for drying malt by the air; a flying engine; a 'night machine', that is, a burglar alarm; a machine for powdering periwigs; a scheme to make salt water fresh; a wheel for perpetual motion; a hospital for illegitimate children (Gulliver would have ranked this among the more 'visionary' plans of the political projectors); a fish-pool (a different scheme from Steele's); and an engine to remove South Sea House to Moorfields, that is, Bedlam. The scatological parts of the academy are matched by one of 156 villainous projects, said to have been turned down by the Privy Council, designed for the purpose of 'inoffensively emptying bog-houses'.[16] Perhaps the most vivid to the imagination of all these wild ideas (it has rightly been termed a 'Swiftian apparatus') was James Puckle's machine gun, omnipresent in Bubble satires. According to the patent specification, it possessed a convenient attachment for firing either round or square cannon balls, 'according to whether the enemy were Christians or Turks'. Puckle later put on the market a patent sword, which he claimed was 'worth a victory to the first army that has it'.[17] There were also the everlasting efforts to discover a reliable way of finding the longitude.[18]

Again we need not suppose that Swift read of all these, let alone the projects for fattening of hogs, the company to discover the land of Ophir,[19] the engine for pulling up trees by the roots, or the plan to import jackasses from Spain. It is simply that such ideas were everywhere during the Bubble mania; and it would be impossible to put such things out of a reader's head in the 1720s. The main semantic component of the word 'projector' (which had very little to do with academic science) ensured that.[20] Equally, the word-frame, described as 'a Project for improving speculative Knowledge by practical and mechanical Operations' has clear contemporary relevance. In 1722 a proposal was made for a society, not unlike the later Royal Society of Arts, which should concern itself with 'operative knowledge', mechanical works, and the like. The author refers to 'many promising Undertakings' which are 'dropt in *Embrio* for Want of Application and Improvement'.[21] There is also a certain affinity to an older invention, the writing engine, enabling one to make several copies of script, 'which had been brought to perfection by the skill of a clock-maker'.[22] This was reported in 1695 in the *Athenian Mercury*, a journal which Swift lauded in its earlier incarnation of the *Athenian Gazette* three years before. The greatest clockwork inventor of this period, however, was undoubtedly Henry Winstanley. He had perished as far back as 1703, when the Great Storm had destroyed his own Eddystone lighthouse. But his widow continued to show his 'water-works' in London as late as 1720, with such attractions as 'the curious Barrel' to entertain spectators. Advertisements were regularly placed in the press, and Swift (who could never resist sights and shows) would have often seen these.[23]

The first book of *Gulliver's Travels* is often linked with the third as utilising 'mechanical' devices to enforce the satire.[24] In this connexion it is interesting to note an echo of contemporary engineering, though on specialised lines, in the voyage to Lilliput. Chapter 5 contains a description of Gulliver's resourceful behaviour when fire threatens the palace at Mildendo. His narrative proceeds in this way:

I found they had already applied Ladders to the Walls of the Apartment, and were well provided with Buckets, but the Water was at some Distance. These Buckets were about the Size of a large Thimble, and the poor People supplied me with them as fast as they could; but the Flame was so violent, that they did little Good ... the Case seemed wholly desperate and deplorable; and this magnificent Palace would have infallibly been burnt down to the Ground, if, by a Presence of Mind, unusual to me, I had not suddenly thought of an Expedient.

He goes on to relate how he had drunk that evening a 'very diuretick' wine called 'glimigrim':

> The Heat I had contracted by coming very near the Flames, and by my labouring to quench them, made the Wine begin to operate by Urine; which I voided in such a Quantity, and applied so well to the proper Places, that in three Minutes the Fire was wholly extinguished; and the rest of that noble Pile, which had cost so many Ages in erecting, preserved from Destruction. (pp. 55-6)

It happens that during the years 1723-5, covering the later part of the writing and revision of *Gulliver's Travels*, fire-fighting achieved a new public prominence. The two leading figures were an emigré chemist named Gottfried Hanckwitz (d. 1741), known as Ambrose Godfrey (who had been employed by Robert Boyle and in 1730 was elected a Fellow of the Royal Society), and Charles Povey (1652?-1743), 'a Person noted for several Projects and Bubbles', as the *Daily Post* termed him in 1723.[25] The rivalry of these two is well caught in Godfrey's pamphlet, *An Account of the New Method of Extinguishing Fires by Explosion and Suffocation* (1724). Godfrey accuses Povey of attempting to impose on the public and to suppress an invention (his own) 'of real and universal Benefit'. He remarks that water-engines have been 'of late brought to such a pitch of Perfection, that by their Means Water may be forced up to a Surprising Height, with almost incredible Swiftness, in a large and continued Stream'. After paying tribute to Mr Boyle, 'the generous Promoter of my Fortune', Godfrey adds in the very accents of the modest proposer: 'I shall pay my self with the inward Satisfaction of having contributed a Mite towards the Publick Good, in making a Discovery of what will tend to the great Advantage even of the latest Posterity.[26]

The 'Introducer' of the scheme, as he calls himself, then relates various practical trials to which he has put his new equipment. The first experiment, in April 1723, proved disastrous, despite the presence of such worthies as the Lord Chancellor, Sir Hans Sloan, and Sir James Thornhill.[22] The ladder caught fire, the engineer 'was oblig'd to quit the Ladder by a fall', and the upper storeys of the test-house were consumed. But a better result was obtained next time, on 30 May 1723, when a site in Westminster Fields was used. Godfrey then proceeds to attack Povey's 'tin bomb', suggeting that its gold lettering and lacquered hoops were the best items, and implying that Povey rigged his own public trials.[28] The controversy went on after the publication of this pamphlet. Another public display was reported in Mist's *Weekly Journal* on 4 December 1725. Here the Performance of 'the new Engine for extinguishing Fire' was described as 'so wonderfully great, by throwing out a vast Quantity of Water in a continued Stream, to such a prodigious Heighth and Distance, and with that great Force, as occasioned a general Approbation of all the Spectators; and, in the Opinion of several very good Judges, is not to be equall'd in Goodness with any other Engine of that Size, and is worked only by four Persons'. One is irresistibly put in mind of the contest in the *Dunciad* to see 'Who best can send on high/The salient spout, far streaming to the sky' (II. 161):

> Not so from shameless Curl; impetuous spread
> The stream, and smoking flourish'd o'er his head.
> ... Swift as it mounts, all follow with their eyes.
> (II. 179–85)

This may seem a little remote from the 'Southern Journey' where we began. But a direct, as well as a symbolic, link can be traced. The *London Journal* reported on 21 December 1723:

> We hear, that the Honourable Directors of the Royal South-Sea Company are so extremely pleas'd with the Performance of the three Water Engines they lately bought of Mr. Newsham, in New-street, Cloth Fair, London, that many of the Quality and Gentry, with Recommendations from them, have since furnished themselves therewith; Sir John Eyles, Bart., Sub-Governor of the said Company, has also bought one for the Defence of his own house and watering his Gardens. The inimitable Performance and Usefulness of the said Engines were published in the Whitehall and St James's Evening Posts on the 7th Inst, whereby it's said, from the compleat Readiness, the little Room they are played in, with great Force and

Distance, and the vast Quantity of Water they play out in each Minute; that the cumbersome squirting Engines which lose much Water, [and] are long in fixing ... will become wholly useless.

The puff concludes with the information that Mr Newsham has now finished constructing 'a prodigious large one' which plays at a distance of forty-five yards.

Newsham was on the respectable fringe of the projecting mania. But the lunatic side, represented by Povey, had its South-Sea connexions—witness Read's *Weekly Journal* of 19 November 1720, just after the collapse of the Bubble:

The famous Mr. Povey, Projector of the half-Penny Post, and other Schemes has now oblig'd the World with one, for making a new Coyn of Gold and Silver, to give in Exchange for South-Sea stock and Paper Money; &c. to be call'd the Royal Coin, and that all Money in the Exchequer and South Sea Company be melted down, and new Coyn'd at a 5th or 10th Part in Weight of the present Species, and be made to pass by Act of Parliament in all publick Revenues and other Payments whatever; to be made from 2s. 6d. Value to 50s. in Silver, and in Gold from 3 pounds to 10. We shall not reflect upon the honest Meaning of this Projector; but I'm afraid if it should make us Rich in our own Eyes, it would make us Poor in the Eyes of our Neighbours.

Had Povey's scheme been feasible, William Wood assuredly would have seen his chance. Swift presents Wood's actual coinages as making for the same sharp devaluation (falsely, however).

As a final point of contact between Scriblerus and the engineers, it might be added that John Rich, that favourite butt of the satirists, had a great deal of trouble with fires around 1724–5, and as well as buying fire buckets and a water-engine had recruited a special team of fire-fighters;[29] at the same time fire insurance was fast developing. Povey was deeply involved here, and other characteristic enthusiasts were Defoe in England and (a little later) Franklin in America.[30]

One of the best known London newspapers of the time, Nathaniel Mist's *Weekly Journal*, often reprinted Swift's work; as a staunchly Tory organ, it seems to have been the favourite paper of the Scriblerians. In the spring of 1723 the idiom of bubbles remained on everyone's lips—a satirical reference in the *London Journal* announced a 'Public Experiment' devised by an engineer, who had invented an 'Engine to pull up the Treasury by the roots'. Often Mist included items of this kind: but his coverage at this juncture included more serious items. One piece of ingenuity was a machine to plough without horses (23 February); two weeks later, on 9 March, came news for all 'honest industrious Farmers':

> A Liquor is propos'd to be sold for the improvement of mean barren Land, either in Corn or Grain, to an incredible Degree, viz. it said one Seed, or Grain of Corn, being first prepared by the said Liquor, will produce from 20 to 70 Ears and upward.

The proposal is recommended to the curious, or 'to those that hath Occasion to make Trial of the Experiment'. The results of such an experiment, if it was ever conducted, have not come down to us. One who would surely have been eager to carry out trials would have been the King of Brobdingnag, who memorably gave it as his opinion that 'whoever could make two Ears of Corn, or two Blades of Grass to grow upon a Spot of Ground, where only one grew before; would deserve better of Mankind, and do more essential Service to his Country, than the whole Race of Politicians put together' (p. 136). In Brobdingnag mathematics is 'wholly applied to what may be useful in Life; to the Improvement of Agriculture and all mechanical Arts'. For Swift crude mechanical experiments may be used to image the reductive operations of politicians: nevertheless, for truly practical 'projects' in the mechanical arts, Swift seems to have had—like Samuel Johnson—nothing but respect.

Again I do not argue (what cannot be demonstrated) that Swift read of these events in time to make direct allusions in the text of *Gulliver's Travels*. Rather, the matter is illustrative. It indicates the kind of engineering project which was precisely contemporaneous with the writing, and suggests the matrix of ideas within which Swift worked. No special assumption is required: simply, we have to accept that Swift kept his ears and eyes open whilst at work on *Gulliver's Travels*. Many critics—with the notable exception of Case—seem to feel that his active assimilative powers had been frozen some years before.

III

Scattered throughout the book are numerous references to engineering. At the outset we learn that the Lilliputians have 'arrived to a great Perfection in Mechanicks by the Countenance and Encouragement of the Emperor, who is a renowned Patron of Learning' (this perhaps a dig at court patronage, directly or indirectly, of men such as Wood). There follows an elaborate description of the 'Operation' mounted to transport Gulliver (pp. 26–7). Lagado, of course, is full of 'engines' such as the word-frame; and building construction is touched on, with the 'most ingenious Architect' working down from roof to foundation (p. 180). But there are passing suggestions elsewhere. In Brobdingnag the King is at first inclined to suppose that Gulliver 'might be a Piece of Clock-work, (which is in that Country arrived to a very great Perfection) contrived by some ingenious Artist' (p. 103). There are baleful overtones to many of these words in the 1720s. An even more interesting example occurs in the sixth chapter of the same voyage, in which Gulliver describes 'Several Contrivances of the Author to please the King and Queen' (p. 125). Most unlike the practical and purposive Robinson Crusoe (though he 'always had a mechanical Genius') Gulliver has been making a tiny comb and 'a neat little Purse . . . more for Shew than Use' (p. 126). He then turns to music, having learnt to play the spinet in his youth. But even this most ethereal art becomes something very unlike Schopenhauer's abstract version: a violent physical exercise, and a matter of 'banging' keys with two cudgels. This is Swift's typical game of bringing down the elevated and ideal to a crude exertion of foot-pounds. Here the reductive effect (and the joke) depends on the tinkly, light-toned spinet—appropriate to Scarlatti, let us say, or Rameau—being appropriated for this galumphing performance. It is as though Swift were dancing with heavy boots upon the tomb of Couperin.

Some of this, no doubt, is to be expected in a book heavily reliant on physical dislocations and transformations of scale. And there seems to be something of that fixative effect noted by Denis Donoghue. Swift, says Donoghue with trenchant accuracy, 'was uneasy with anything that did not occupy space.[31] But beyond all this is the fact that technology was a leading agent of innovation in Swift's lifetime, and that engineers were among the purest expressions of the projecting spirit. A.E. Case seems to me abundantly justified in the climactic importance he gives to the South Sea affair:

> Swift must have seen in this catastrophe the justification of his own political theories and the opportunity for his reentry into the larger world of European affairs. He begins to show renewed interest in his English public in the fall of 1720: quite possibly we may date the conception of Gulliver early in that fall, when the significance of the South Sea debacle was becoming evident.[32]

To this I would add only that Gulliver's 'Southern Journey' is placed in its full historic perspective when we look at the doings of speculators, engineers, inventors, and company promoters. *Gulliver's Travels* may have entered the history of ideas, thanks mainly to the Houyhnhnms and Yahoos. But it *derives* not just from a course of philosophic reading, but from a lively engagement in contemporary life, and a ready exposure to the popular news-stories of the day.

Notes

1. Swift *Corr*, III, 6.
2. Ricardo Quintana, *Swift: An Introduction* (London, 1955), pp. 146-7. For the view that *Gulliver's Travels* derives in a fairly direct way from earlier Scriblerian ventures, see *The Memoirs of Martin Scriblerus*, ed Charles Kerby-Miller (New Haven, Connecticut, 1950), pp. 50-53, 315-20. My own view is closer to that of Arthur E. Case, *Four Essays on Gulliver's Travels* (Princeton, New Jersey, 1950), pp. 97-107.
3. Quotations follow Swift *Prose*, Vol. XI. Page references are placed in the text within brackets. For references to South Sea affairs, see the index to *Prose* and *Corr*. For Swift's poem 'The Bubble', see *Corr*, II, 365.

   I should like to record my gratitude to Mr J.M. Treadwell for many stimulating suggestions and valuable items of information. He is not responsible for the detailed conclusions reached, but his own wider study of Swift and contemporary projectors has afforded me a number of insights.

   For a quasi—South Sea episode which had come to Swift's attention, see the account of Coleire's adventures in Treadwell, 'Swift, Richard Coleire and *Gulliver's Travels*', *RES*, XXXIV (1983), 304-11.
4. *The Voyage to Cacklogallinia* (1727) interpreted *Gulliver* in the aftermath of the Bubble: see the edition by Marjorie Hope Nicolson (New York, 1940).

5. Case, pp. 87-9, identifies Munodi with Robert Harley, and the mill as 'the old English fiscal system'. Munodi's family is 'the British empire', and the club of projectors 'Defoe and his abettors'. The new mill is the South Sea Company, the agitated water is 'money put into active circulation by speculation', and so on. Perhaps this is to make the allegory spuriously precise, but it seems to me overwhelmingly likely that Swift had the Bubble and its attendant mania in mind here. I depart from Case in emphasising the general 'projecting' and engineering drift of the allegory. For Swift on Burnet and the development of public credit, see *Prose*, VII, 68; and (using the term 'Projector') VI, 10.

6. Carswell, pp. 14-16: Case, p. 89: Defoe, *Tour*, I, 357-8. Defoe cites at length a 'Scheme' for rebuilding the palace, costed by an unnamed 'Undertaker' (pp. 358-64). Note also Carswell's imagery; 'Until the Revolution the old reservoirs still seemed big enough to contain the new floods of wealth ... in the years immediately following the Revolution pent-up wealth and initiative burst their banks' (pp. 9-10).

7. Defoe, *Tour*, II, 562-3. For the identification of Sorocold and other details, see my abridged edition of the *Tour* (Harmondsworth, 1971), p. 711. For Boswell's comments on a visit to the Lombe silk-mills in September 1777, see *Boswell in Extremes 1776-78*, ed. C.M. Weiss and F.A. Pottle (New Haven and London, 1971), pp. 163-4. For Johnson's similar remarks in July 1774, see *The Works of Samuel Johnson*, Vol. I, *Diaries, Prayers, and Annals*, ed. E.L. McAdam, Jr, Donald and Mary Hyde (New Haven, Connecticut, 1958), p. 170.

8. These two paragraphs are based chiefly on L.T.C. Rolt, *Thomas Newcomen: The Prehistory of the Steam Engine* (Dawlish and London, 1963), supplemented by official sources such as the *Journal of the House of Lords*. For the satire in Read's paper, see Thomas Wright, *Caricature History of the Georges* (London, n.d.), pp. 45-8.

9. On the York Buildings Company, see my edition of the *Tour*, p. 719. On Billingsley, see Carswell, pp. 167-8; F.B. Relton, *An Account of the Fire Insurance Companies... also of Charles Povey* (London, 1893), pp. 121, 153; Barry Supple, *The Royal Exchange Assurance* (Cambridge, 1970), pp. 12-13, 33-4. Other water works were developed at this time, notably one at Shadwell.

10. Public Record Office, London, SP 35/50/5. The previous year he had found London too hot and had decamped to the Continent, where the press avidly followed his movements—*London Journal*, 23 February; *Freeholder's Journal*, 6 March 1723.

11. For Newsham, see PRO, SP 35/29/18, SP 35/56/8, SP 44/253/10, 15, 552: *Daily Post*, 7 May 1720. A typical Wood application can be seen in SP 44/252/223-6. For a general account of the projector's career, see J.M. Treadwell, 'Swift, William Wood, and the factual basis of satire', *Journal of British Studies*, XV (1976), 76-91; and 'William Wood and the Company of Ironmasters of Great Britain', *Business History*, XVI (1974), 97-112.

12. PRO, SP 35/20/62b, SP 35/25/96, SP 35/30/36, SP 35/31/71, SP 35/45/11, SP 35/48/84, SP 35/49/18, 25, 34, SP 35/50/19, SP 35/51/31, SP 35/62/84. Another allied venture was the recovery of wrecked ships, in

which the grand speculator Thomas Neale had been involved (as had Defoe). More improbable was the association of a highly respectable under-secretary, Charles Delafaye (known to Swift): SP 35/30/24, Other 'diving' projects are mentioned in SP 35/21/105 and elsewhere. I am indebted to Mr Treadwell for some of these references.

13. Rolt, p. 85; F.G. Stephens, *Catalogue of Prints and Drawings in the British Museum . . . Political and Personal Satires*, 11 vols (London, 1873), II, 432.

14. For a typical complaint of breach of patent in 'two very useful machines' by 'some of the Town Projectors', see PRO, SP 35/26/4 (1 April 1721).

15. Marjorie Nicolson and Nora M. Mohler, 'The scientific background of Swift's *Voyage to Laputa*', *Annals of Science*, 2 (1937), 299–334. Case's reservations about the predominantly scientific nature of the satire are healthy (p. 89).

16. Projects drawn from press notices, and from Wright, pp. 42–59; Carswell, pp. 141–2; Stephens, pp. 431–2; and PRO, SP 35, various bundles. Case (pp. 90–91) offers a highly selective list; the only reference he supplies is to the outdated and shallow monograph, Lewis Melville, *The South Sea Bubble* (London, 1921). Subsequent works to which Case did not have access (notably Carswell and P.G.M. Dickson, *The Financial Revolution in England 1688–1760* (London, 1967)) provide abundant confirmatory detail.

17. The description 'Swiftian' comes from Peter Quennell, *Caroline of England* (London, 1939), p. 94. See also Carswell, pp. 76, 142; Stephens, p. 429.

18. See for instance PRO, SP 35/5/68.

19. Read's *Weekly Journal*, 16 July 1720.

20. Case points this out (p. 90); what he says is certainly correct, but if anything he understates his argument.

21. D.G.C. Allan, *William Shipley: Founder of the Royal Society of Arts* (London, 1968), pp. 10, 163–8.

22. David Ogg, *England in the Reigns of James II and William III* (Oxford, 1955), pp. 39–40.

23. See for example *Daily Post*, 13 May 1720: *Daily Courant*, 12 September 1720. On the popularity of Winstanley's water-works, see John Ashton, *Social Life in the Reign of Queen Anne* (London, 1883), pp. 219–21.

24. For example, Angus Ross's edition of *Gulliver's Travels* (London, 1872), p. 311.

25. Quoted by Relton, p. 530, in what is still the standard account of Povey. For Godfrey, see also PRO, SP/35/75/36. (There are other water-engines in SP 35/56/8 and SP 35/58/105.) The controversy between Povey and Godfrey, and their various public trials, can be followed in the *Daily Post* and *Daily Journal* from May to July 1723.

26. Godfrey, *Account of the New Method* (London, 1724), pp. iii–iv, xi, xvi.

27. Thornhill's presence is interesting in view of the use made by his son-in-law, Hogarth, of fire-fighting as a satiric motif. For a good example, see Ronald Paulson, *Hogarth: His Life, Art, and Times*, 2 vols (New Haven, 1971), II, 359. It is odd that the Prince of Wales (later George II) had something of a mania for attending fires (see Relton, p. 420).

28. Godfrey, pp. 4–6, 21–9. Godfrey states his desire to produce something 'truly Beneficial to my Fellow-Subjects' and stresses the 'Reasonableness'

of his method (p. 15). Godfrey was probably responsible for a mock-theatrical advertisement concerning 'the Farce' of 'the Belsize Projector' in the *Daily Journal* of 15 July 1723.

29.   *The London Stage 1660–1800*, 5 vols in 11, Part II, 1700–1729, ed. Emmett L. Avery (Carbondale, Illinois, 1960), pp. l–li.

30.   Arthur M. Schlesinger, *The Birth of the Nation* (New York, 1969), pp. 102–3.

31.   Denis Donoghue, *Jonathan Swift: A Critical Introduction* (Cambridge, 1969), p. 131.

32.   Case, pp. 106–7. The South Sea mania did affect Ireland, whence Bishop Nicolson reported that all money had been swallowed up by Exchange Alley. There followed a liquidity crisis, and the shortage of specie which occasioned the grant of Wood's patent to coin halfpennies. In fact, the great 'project' at the centre of the Drapier's Letters was an indirect byproduct of the Bubble. See further Dickson, pp. 140, 158.

3

'DOG-LOGICK' IN SWIFT'S *UPON THE HORRID PLOT*

Miss. I'd have you to know I scorn your Words.
Neverout. Well, ay but scornful Dogs, they say, will eat dirty Puddings.

Swift, *Polite Conversation*, (Swift *Prose*, IV, 140)

I

The recent growth of interest in Swift's poetry has not so far brought with it a proportionate increase in the range of his work discussed. For the most part the familiar poems have remained at the centre of critical attention. Readings abound of *Verses on the Death of Dr Swift*, *Cadenus and Vanessa*, and the *Description of a City Shower*. It is true that the early odes are now receiving more notice, and one can observe an occasional poem moving into a more prominent position: thus, *Vanbrug's House* has provoked a lengthy discussion in two of the full-length monographs which have lately appeared.[1] But none of these books pays any heed to a characteristic and, in my view, important area of Swift's work as a poet. This is the witty commentary on topical issues, represented by *The Virtues of Sid Hamet's Rod* (1710), *A Dialogue Between Captain Tom and Sir Henry Dutton Colt* (1710), and *A Serious Poem upon William Wood* (1724). Perhaps there is a lingering feeling that such 'topical' pieces are best approached in terms of their subject-matter: that they belong in heavily annotated editions of *Poems on Affairs of State*, and yield comparatively little when subjected to minute critical analysis.

My feeling is quite the reverse. These poems exhibit some of Swift's most pointed and forceful writing. Although less 'personal' than certain poems, and less capable of psychoanalytic

29

interpretation, they show immense literary skills deployed on topics which were profoundly important to Swift. They illustrate his habits of thought and his techniques of composition as well as any works in the canon. Swift wrote not far short of three hundred English poems, and if we want to understand his general working methods this group of poems provides many valuable clues. In addition, they offer a number of direct links with the prose works, and illuminate a wider range of Swiftian texts than, say, the scatological poems appear to do.

The particular example I wish to discuss is moderately well known, but it has never been discussed in depth. It is a poem of 76 lines concerned with the Atterbury episode, written presumably in 1722 and first published in Faulkner's notable edition of 1735. There is unlikely to be any dispute on the fact that Swift cared deeply about the fate of Atterbury as an individual and about the fate of his cause. Whether or not Swift had any concealed sympathy for the Jacobite movement (as the ministry long supposed), he was certainly an agonised observer of what G.V. Bennett has called 'the Tory crisis in church and state'.[2] The exact nature of his interest in the Atterbury affair (manifest in *Gulliver's Travels*) is the subject of a fine essay by Edward W. Rosenheim, Jr., and it is unnecessary to labour this point any further.[3] My aim is rather to show how Swift devised an original technique to express his view of the arrest and trial of his friend. There is in my submission one clear key to the imaginative workings of this poem. *Upon the Horrid Plot* is quite simply built around a chain of proverbs, linked together almost like a string of sausages.

II

Everyone knows that Swift had a well-developed interest in proverbs, maxims, popular tags, folk expressions and the like. Its most obvious product was the dictionary of received ideas he compiled, which we are familiar with under the title of *Polite Conversation*. Some years ago a debate took place on the status of the proverbs scattered through this work. Mackie L. Jarrell argued that they were drawn from the many collections of proverbs published in the seventeenth and early eighteenth centuries.[4] Subsequently David Hamilton replied to this case, and sought to demonstrate that this was an unnecessary and unsupported assumption.[5] Another relevant contribution was made by George P. Mayhew, who showed that Swift probably made his most concentrated effort on *Polite Conversation* in two bursts, around 1731-2 and 1734-6.[6] But it is agreed that the work had been planned and begun at an earlier stage, though neither Mayhew nor anyone else can specify exactly when.

It is immediately apparent that Swift's interest in proverbial lore antedates by many years the periods just mentioned. More than that, it can be shown that Swift had evolved ways of exploiting this interest in verse, at least as early as 1710. The *Dialogue between Captain Tom and Colt* ends in a battery of proverbs;[7] whilst a poem such as *The Fable of Midas* (1712) constantly hovers around this area of expression.[8] Moreover, there is striking evidence in a poem generally attributed to Swift, *The Fable of the Bitches* (1715).[9] It has escaped the attention of all editors that the meaning of this poem depends on an unstated Scottish proverb (the piece concerns Scottish politics after the Union), that is, 'Bourd not with Bawtie lest he bite you.' If Swift did write this fable—as editors from Faulkner in 1762 to Sir Harold Williams have readily accepted—then he was capable of making direct *structural* use of proverb lore.

When we turn to the text of *Upon the Horrid Plot*, we find only one explicit recognition of what is going on:

> *Tory.* Why then the Proverb is not right,
> Since you can *teach dead Dogs to bite.*
>
> (39-40)

The italics are a reliable indication, in such a context, of some kind of allusion or verbal play. We now know that Swift took considerable care with the copy that went to the printer for the 1735 edition, and accidentals are more likely to be significant here than in any other branch of his writing. It is therefore prudent to look at the other passages in this poem where italics are employed. Disregarding their use for names such as '*Oates*' or *Mason*' (and the speech prefixes for the interlocutors, '*Whig*' and '*Tory*'), they figure on about twelve or thirteen occasions. It should be noted that the word *Dog* regularly appears in italics: in fact, on nineteen of its twenty appearances. To an alert reader, when the poem first appeared in 1735, this was a heavy nudge; we are to expect some kind of linguistic byplay surrounding dogs.

The form which this byplay takes can be briefly stated. Williams does not normally record in his notes the source or even the presence of proverbial expressions. (He does not even do this at 1.40, where the nature of the phrase is pointed out in the text.) In fact, it emerges that at least twelve proverbs are quoted or alluded to in the poem, almost all of them explicitly concerned with dogs. They can be traced in older collections and docketed with a precise identification in a modern compilation such as that of Morris P. Tilley.[10] That is to say, the expressions in question were undeniably of a proverbial cast, long familiar to a wide audience. It is possible to enter into debate as to the use Swift makes of this circumstance; but the basic fact is demonstrable in precise detail. And I would contend that we cannot penetrate the inner meaning of the poem until we have fully grasped this point. Otherwise we shall be left with Elrington Ball's limp comments, and find no way into the poem's literary effects.[11]

It will be recalled that *Upon the Horrid Plot* originates in the use of a dog named Harlequin in the trial of Atterbury before the House of Lords. As J.H. Plumb describes it:

> The conspirators tripped themselves up in spite of an elaborate use of fictitious names and cyphers—the break was provided by a little spotted dog called Harlequin, about whose injuries and movements everyone was willing to sign confessions, either forgetting or being ignorant, that the dog had been referred to in the treasonable correspondence. Harlequin had been sent as a present to Atterbury's wife from France; once established, this proved that *Jones* and *Illingworth* were cover names for Atterbury.[12]

The Tories regarded it as unjust that the ministry had proceeded against Atterbury through the rare and somewhat technical device of a 'bill of pains and penalties'; they suspected that an ordinary prosecution in the courts would have failed for lack of evidence. In addition, Swift nurtured a lifelong hatred for informers, as *Gulliver's Travels* illustrates. What happens in the poem is that the use of the dog Harlequin is treated as symbolic for the whole range of state investigation and surveillance (something Swift had himself undergone). At a primary level, then, the poem constitutes a critique of the forensic methods employed by the Walpole government.

III

When the word 'dog' first appears in the text, an untutored reader might easily suppose (as Tory affects to do) that this is a contemptuous expression for a vile human being:

> I ask'd a *Whig* the other Night,
> How came this wicked Plot to Light:
> He answer'd that a *Dog* of late
> Informed a Minister of State.   (1-4)

At the outset Swift identifies ministers of state with low wretches, and this connection is strengthened rather than weakened as the poem proceeds. Whig explains that he did not refer to a 'perjured *Dog*', which 'denotes' a corrupt informer such as Titus Oates (9-10). He meant a real live dog. He adds, 'But you must know this Dog was lame' (12) which was actually the case: Harlequin had been injured in transit from France to England. To this Tory can make the sharp retort, 'Your *Evidence* was lame' (14); the italics indicate a pun, which depends on the old meaning of 'evidence'—a witness.[13] It also makes for an easy transference to the first dog-proverb: 'Come, help your *lame Dog o'er the Style.*' (15)
Like most of these expressions, the phrase 'lame dog' is usually applied to a person,[14] and the allusion works to reinforce our sense of Atterbury's prosecutors as petty and corrupt. Whig insists that Harlequin is indeed only an animal:

> I mean a *Dog*, without a Joke,
> Can howl, and bark, but never spoke.   (17-18)

The second line carries rich implications, but the central thought might be expressed along these lines: 'The most damaging witness the prosecution could summon was a whining little dog, incapable of giving real oral testimony.'
    At this point Tory extends the canine reference by referring to

other witnesses as 'Curr *Plunket*' and 'Whelp *Skean*', together
described as 'An *English* or an *Irish* Hound' (20–1). Words such as
cur or even *whelp* retain some pejorative sense in modern usage,
but we have probably forgotten that *hound* once carried strong
hostile overtones: *OED* gives the meaning 'a detested, mean, or
despicable man'.[15] The opprobrious intent is more obvious in the
next two lines:

> Or t'other Puppy that was drown'd,
> Or *Mason* that abandon'd Bitch.   (22–3)

Rosenheim has shown that Swift in all probability confused
certain of the names here,[16] but from the point of view of his
satiric strategy that is of no consequence. What is happening is
clear: the prosecution case is being portrayed as reliant on low
and disreputable persons, resembling not so much the toy lapdog
Harlequin as the scruffiest mongrel picking at refuse in the alleys.
Their testimony is worth nothing, for 'all the Noise they made
was *barking*' (26).

The charge now shifts to that of suborning the witnesses. In a
passage constructed round a whole series of proverbs, Tory sets
out Swift's accusations concerning the way Walpole mounted the
prosecution:

> You pay them well; the *Dogs* have got
> Their *Dogs-heads in a Porridge-pot:*
> And 'twas but just; for, wise Men say,
> That, *every Dog must have his Day.*
> *Dog W*(alpole) laid a Quart of *Nog* on 't,
> He'd either *make a Hog or Dog on 't,*
> And look't since he has got his Wish,
> As if he had *thrown down a Dish.*
> Yet, this I dare foretel you from it,
> He'll soon *return to his own Vomit.*   (27–36)

The first saying, in ll. 27–8, refers to the old proverb 'the dog (or
hog) is got into the porridge pot'—we might say, 'they have got
on to the gravy train', or some equivalent.[17] The expression in l.
30 is more familiar: significantly, it is one of the clichés exposed in
Polite Conversation.[18] It is noteworthy that Swift often likes to
appeal to popular wisdom (or pretend to do so) with a formula

such as 'wise Men say'. In 1. 31, Walpole is introduced with the
appellation '*Dog*'; nog is strong beer which came, like the prime
minister, from Norfolk. The proverb quoted in 1. 32 meant 'to
bring a thing to one use or another', that is, to find some kind of
advantage in the available means at one's disposal.[19] It may be
added that hog and dog were both cant words for coins (Swift
himself uses the latter in his *Drapier's Letters*),[20] and thus they
reinforce the sense of a bribe or pay-off. In 1. 34 the italicised
expression is for once not found in dictionaries of proverbs, but it
evidently carries on the theme of an animal glutting itself. One
thinks of the phrase 'not a word to throw at a dog', which occurs
in *Polite Conversation*. The final couplet alludes aptly enough to the
Book of Proverbs, xxvi, 11—whence of course the saying had of
course entered general usage.[21]

Whig retorts by pointing out that the discovery of the plot was
helped by the deposition of Philip Neynoe; this deposition was
used after Neynoe had been drowned whilst attempting to escape
from custody. But the phrase used—'found/By *Neno* after he was
drown'd' (37-8) plays into Tory's hands, for it again suggests a
hapless doglike fate (drowned like an unwanted puppy), and
even suggests it may have been convenient for the prosecution
that Neynoe should have died at that juncture. Then comes the
couplet I quoted earlier on, concerning dead dogs.[22] Whig replies
by asserting once more that the principal agent of the
prosecution is 'a real *Curr*,/A *Dog* of Spirit for his Years' (44-5).
His attributes include 'two hanging Ears': pendulous, but by
inescapable contemporary connotation implying also 'worthy of
being hanged'.

Then follows:

> His Name is Harlequin, I wot,
> And that's a Name in every *Plot*.   (47-8)

There is a lot going on in little verbal space here. Harlequin was
of course the dog's name; the second line refers to the activities of
the intriguer in *commedia dell' arte*—the poem was written as a new
pantomime form gained popularity under titles such as *Harlequin
Sheppard* and *Harlequin Dr Faustus*, produced at Lincoln's Inn
Fields by the impresario John Rich. (Curiously, Rich himself
often danced in the guise of a dog during these 'harlequinades',

he was also widely thought to be illiterate.) The simple doggy associations are important, however: a few years later the poem *Bounce to Fop* refers (1. 40) to 'motley, squinting *Harlequini's*'. This work was originally stated on its appearance in 1736 to have been by Swift. Later editors have suspected that Pope revised the text, and indeed it is now excluded from the standard edition of Swift's *Poems*. Elsewhere I have argued that *Bounce to Fop* in its main lines was probably composed by Swift; one relevant piece of evidence (out of very many pieces not assembled here) is that the poem quotes, four lines earlier, the proverb used in *Upon the Horrid Plot*, 1. 30.[23] Harlequin had actually become the name for an entire breed of spotted dog (perhaps because of the publicity in 1722), and it stayed in the Scriblerian lexicon into the 1730s. After this, Whig ends his speech by describing Harlequin's testimony, 'Confess't as plain as he could bark;/Then with his Fore-foot set his *Mark*' (55–6). The last italicised word puns on 'set one's mark' (used of those who could not sign their name) and 'left his traces' (used of animals). Again the testimony is reduced to that of an animal scratching the earth, or at best an illiterate's muddled confession.

Tory pretends that this has clarified some obscure points:

> Then all this while I have been bubbled;
> I thought it was a *Dog in Doublet*:
> The Matter now no longer sticks;
> For Statesmen never want *Dog-tricks*.   (57–60)

The expression in 1. 58 was proverbial for 'inappropriately proud'; that in 1. 60 for 'low or scurvy tricks' (both are found in Tilley).[24] Tory has now accepted that it was indeed 'a real *Curr*'—a low wretch indeed (Walpole)—who procured Atterbury's conviction. Tory says that Harlequin is not 'a *Dog* in Metaphor', but of course he has served a quasi-metaphoric function. By insisting on the proverbial overtones of the dog, Swift has made a symbolic identification of the prosecutors, disreputable human beings and the whole race of dogs.

Next, Tory reports a rumour that Harlequin is to be given a place at court, where such tools of the ministry will be welcome. He is to be offered the place of turnspit in the royal kitchen—a sneer at the system of patronage in which sinecures of little utility were disposed to compliant men and women. Dogs really were used to pull round a turnspit; however, the thrust here is against place-seeking and (for the first time) against the Hanoverian regime itself. Whig goes on to explain that it was necessary to trump up a plot, presumably to divert the public's mind from ministerial wrongdoing, and goes on:

> And, when we found the *Dog* begin it,
> We guess't the *B*(ishop)'s *Foot was in it.*   (69–70)

This is one of Swift's neatest strokes. In l. 70 he draws on the proverbial phrase, 'the bishop has set his foot in it', used of burning a dish in the kitchen. Swift employed this saying elsewhere in his verse (*A Panegyrick on the Dean*, l. 173), and again it turns up in *Polite Conversation*.[25] The bishop here, of course, is Atterbury himself. What the lines suggest is that the notoriously inflammatory Atterbury was a convenient scapegoat, once the Jacobite scare had been set up. We might paraphrase this section, 'Once we had cooked up the whole affair, we found it easy to suggest that Atterbury had stoked up the rebellion.'

Tory acknowledges that it was a 'dangerous Project' (the noun was particularly baneful, two years after the bursting of the South Sea Bubble, with its attendant frauds). He concedes that Whig has proved his case 'by *Dog-Logick*' (71–2). This last phrase had the sense of 'bad or spurious reasoning',[26] and was used to this end in the *Examiner*. If not quite a proverb this time, the expression assuredly has the ring of folk wisdom. Following this, we move to the savage conclusion:

> Sure such Intelligence between
> A *Dog* and *B*(ishop) ne'er was seen,
> Till you began to change the Breed;
> Your *B*(ishop)*s* all are *D*(o)*gs* indeed.   (73–6)

This refers to the safe appointments made to the episcopal bench made by Walpole, through the agency of Edmund Gibson, Bishop of London. During Walpole's period of power scarcely any but the most loyal Whigs were appointed bishops, and indeed since the Hanoverian accession in 1714 the bench had grown steadily more tractable from the government's point of

view. Swift had seen his own claims, and those of other notable
Tory divines, set aside in favour of appointees such as Benjamin
Hoadly, Samuel Peploe and others. The case became
particularly clear in 1723, when six bishoprics became vacant,
and Walpole and Gibson 'by judicious translations ... advanced
nine whig churchmen up the ladder of episcopal preferment'.[27]
But throughout his reign Walpole depended on the bishops to
come to his aid in Parliament, and in time he could rely on
twenty-four of the twenty-six votes they exercised in the Lords.

It is not hard to see the drift of this endling. Walpole has
'changed the breed' of churchmen, by appointing men on
political rather than religious grounds. Dogs and bishops from
now on will find it easy to communicate with one another, for
church and state are now run by dogs in the sense of *OED*, 3a: 'a
worthless, despicable ... or cowardly fellow'. By sustained
allusion to a body of proverbial wisdom, Swift has established a
strong connection between Atterbury's adverseries (the
machinery of state repression, as Swift sees it) and the worst kind
of curlike behaviour. Of course, politically he may have been in
the wrong: there really was a Jacobite conspiracy, Atterbury
really was involved, the Harlequin evidence really did mean
what it was alleged to mean, and so on. But that scarcely affects
the brilliance of Swift's literary technique.

Upon the Horrid Plot is interesting because it does in a highly
concentrated form things that Swift did repeatedly, but in most
cases more dispersedly, in his verse. The overlap with *Polite
Conversation* which occurs here can be found in at least forty of his
poems. Similarly, the use made here of actual, so to speak
'registered', proverbs can be paralleled by the use of less
formulaic cliché in works such as *The Journal of a Modern Lady*
(1729), or the use of conversational commonplace in *The Grand
Question Debated* (1729). We are now readier to accept punning as
a significant resource in Swift's satiric armoury.[28] There is some
punning, for that matter, in *Upon the Horrid Plot*: but its main
device is the systematic conversion of proverbs into belittling
allusions. What the poem says, subliminally, is: the real dirty
dogs are Walpole and his instruments. Its inner dynamic is a
cogent '*Dog-logick*', assembled not from ordinary propositions but
from one dog-proverb piled upon another.[29]

Notes

1. John Irwin Fischer, *On Swift's Poetry* (Gainesville, Florida, 1978), pp. 75–95; Peter J. Schakel, *The Poetry of Jonathan Swift* (Madison, Wisconsin, 1978), pp. 29–42.
2. G.V. Bennett, *The Tory Crisis in Church and State 1688–1730* (Oxford, 1975), describes Atterbury's career in the context of political and religious struggles of the period.
3. Edward Rosenheim, 'Swift and the Atterbury Case', *The Augustan Milieu*, ed. H.K. Miller *et al.* (Oxford, 1970), pp. 174–204. Rosenheim mentions *Upon the Horrid Plot* briefly, pp. 175, 190. Swift's title may derive from a proceedings, when Pulteney moved a 'question' that 'there had been a horrid and detestable conspiracy': see *The Parliamentary Diary of Sir Edward Knatchbull*, ed. A.N.Newman (London, 1963), p. 15.
4. Mackie L. Jarrell, 'The Proverbs in Swift's *Polite Conversation*', *HLQ*, XX (1956), 15–38.
5. David Hamilton, 'Swift, Wagstaff, and the composition of *Polite Conversation*', *HLQ*, XXX (1967), 281–95.
6. George P. Mayhew, 'Swift's Anglo-Latin games and a fragment of *Polite Conversation*', *HLQ*, XVII (1954), 133–59); reprinted in *Rage or Raillery* (San Marino, California, 1967), pp. 131–55.
7. See Frank H. Ellis (ed.), *Poems on Affairs of State* (New Haven, 1963–75), VII, 486.
8. See Swift *Poems* I, 156–8. All quotations and references follow this edition.
9. Swift *Poems*, I, 207–09. Other evidence of an early 'critical' attitude to proverbs is found in a letter to Ambrose Philips, dating from 1708: *Corr*, I, 91. See also 'Swift and the Reanimation of Cliché', *The Character of Swift's Satire: A Revised Focus*, ed. Claude Rawson (Newark, N.J., 1983), pp. 203–26.
10. Morris P. Tilley, *A Dictionary of the Proverbs in England in the Sixteenth and Seventeenth Centuries* (Ann Arbor, Michigan, 1950). References are to 'Tilley', followed by the entry number.
11. F. Elrington Ball, *Swift's Verse* (London, 1928; reprinted New York, 1970), p. 167. As elsewhere, Ball shows little interest in the literary—as opposed to the factual—aspect of Swift's poems.
12. J.H. Plumb, *Sir Robert Walpole: The King's Minister* (London, 1960), pp. 43–4.
13. *OED*, 'evidence', *sb.*, 7. Another meaning listed in this paragraph is 'spy'. *OED* lists sense 7 as obsolete, but it was still current and indeed common in Swift's day.
14. Tilley D479. This proverb also turns up in *Polite Conversation*: see Swift, *Prose* IV, 155.
15. *OED*, 'hound', *sb.*¹, 4.
16. Rosenheim, 'Swift and the Atterbury Case', p. 191.
17. Tilley H491.
18. Tilley D464; Swift *Prose*, IV, 182.
19. Tilley H496.
20. *The Drapier's Letters*, ed. Herbert Davis (Oxford, 1935), p. 43.

21. Tilley W762, D455: Swift, *Prose*, IV, 134. Compare also *a Tale of a Tub*: 'A *True Critick* is like a *Dog* at a feast, whose Thoughts and Stomach are wholly set upon what the Guests *fling away*!

22. Swift apparently conflates two sayings: 'You cannot teach an old dog new tricks,' and 'Dead dogs do not bite.' See Tilley D448.

23. The modern attribution to Pope rests chiefly on a study by Norman Ault, 'Pope and his Dogs', *New Light on Pope* (London, 1949; rptd Hamden, Connecticut, 1967), 337–50. '*Harlequini*'s' became '*Harvequini*'s' in some early editions, a patent thrust at Lord Hervey.

24. Tilley D452 and D546. For 'dog trick', see also *Hudibras*, I. iii. 8.

25. Tilley B406; Swift *Prose*, IV, 134.

26. *OED*, 'dog', *sb.*, 17e. *OED* cites as a usage by Swift the *Examiner* for 19 July 1711. However, though reprinted by Faulkner in 1738, the paper is almost certainly by Mrs Manley (Swift *Prose*, III, xxvii).

27. W.A. Speck, *Stability and Strife: England 1714–1760* (London, 1977), p. 210. This fact may suggest that the ending of the poem relates to 1723 or even 1724 rather than 1722; we have no evidence on the exact date of composition, although the bitter tone may suggest that Atterbury's fate was already sealed. Faulkner's heading 'Written in the Year 1722' may or may not be accurate; he is often wrong in such cases.

28. See David Nokes, '"Hack at Tom Poley's": Swift's Use of Puns', *The Art of Jonathan Swift*, ed. C. Probyn (London, 1978), pp. 43–56.

29. Swift's awareness in this area is confirmed by a reference in a letter to the Duke of Dorset on 30 December 1735, where he quotes from Scripture, 'Although the Childrens meat must not be given to Dogs; yet the Dogs eat the Scraps that fall from the Childrens tables' (*Corr*, IV, 450). The text, not identified by Williams, is either Matthew xv, 26–7, or Mark vii, 27–8. A useful approach to the general issue is W.B. Carnochan, 'Notes on Swift's Proverb Lore', *YES*, VI (1976), 63–9.

4

POPE'S RAMBLES

The urge towards self-exploration figured strongly in the Augustan world. As A.R. Humphreys finely puts it, 'the great houses were not only private residences but showplaces to be publicised by admiring tourists and artists (the eighteenth century is the first great age of guide-books and scenic drawings)'.[1] Suitably for an epoch much addicted to definition, boundary-beating and enclosure, men and women began to make their own survey of Britain. They witnessed at first hand what previous generations had left to specialist authorities, and topography moved from the hands of antiquaries or civil servants into those of travellers and trippers. 'The common sightseer or connoisseur was the effective public for a lot of artistic activity,' Humphreys points out: more and more art presumed what might be called a speculative audience, who might arrive casually on the day, rather than a prepacked court gathering. Everyone knew who was to attend a masque at Ludlow Castle in 1634; practically anyone could (and did) turn up at Shakespearian festivities in Stratford not much more than a century later. And as people became more mobile, the pleasures of scenery were attached to local piety, property and the order of rural society. Where Leland had seen remnants of a battle-scarred feudal world, the eighteenth-century traveller saw views—and views inescapably meant the present day and the current owner, even where Sanderson Miller or one of his kind had been brought in to supply an evocative ruin.

The picturesque moment may have dawned after Pope's death, but the taste for inland journeys started in the high Augustan era.[2] The most famous travellers of this early period are generally regarded as businesslike rather than aesthetic in their outlook, whether local historians like Ralph Thoresby,

41

mettlesome explorers like Celia Fiennes (that adventurous *ur-*Victorian), or journalists and compilers like Defoe or John Macky. It is this obsessive concern with the real world which finds expression in Defoe's *Tour*: although, as we shall see in Chapter 9, something more than straightforward 'realism' is involved. Nevertheless the first quarter of the new century already brought its crop of travellers, as it were, for the sake of it—people who went about the country for private and arbitrary reasons, who took holidays on the road, who set out to test a theory or to win a bet. Camden's *Britannia* was translated, re-edited, abridged, augmented, modernised, beset by rivals actual and potential. It is a profound mistake to think that tourism was simply a child of the picturesque movement. Long before the Lakes were in fashion, people made their peregrination of the northern counties. Half a century before Tintern and Llangollen came into their own, there was a tourist itinerary based on Blenheim, Castle Howard and Wilton. Mansions like Houghton and Holkham became objects of pilgrimage as soon as they were half up: Charles Lyttelton, a bishop who was also a Fellow of the Royal Society and a noted antiquarian, wrote to Sanderson Miller in 1758 that 'very few strangers' would visit a county as unattractive as Norfolk if it had not been for the showplaces in its northern half.[3] For the genteel, a round of country houses and (even more important) their gardens was a well-established custom at a time when the beautiful remained in assured dominance over the sublime or the picturesque.

I

It is not surprising that Alexander Pope, even so early, should exhibit many full-blown characteristics of the tourist. With his fanatical dedication to the art of landscape gardening, he possessed one prime qualification. A connoisseur's interest in the visual arts gave him the awareness of *contemporary* architecture which was an appropriate ingredient at this period. On the other hand, his weakness for 'romantic' moods allowed him to anticipate in some measure the mid-century taste for evocative twilight scenery and Gothic (not yet truly Gothick) appurtenances. Moreover, his feeling for the loss and mutability of things was deeply implanted in his instincts as a writer: it derived from Virgil rather than from currently modish verses on the ruins of Rome. The poet who could compose a passage such as this needed little instruction in the proper technique of musing over broken pillars:

> All vast Possessions (just the same the case
> Whether you call them Villa, Park, or Chase)
> Alas, my BATHURST! what will they avail?
> Join *Cotswold* Hills to *Saperton's* fair Dale,
> Let rising Granaries and Temples here,
> There mingled Forms and Pyramids appear,
> Link Towns to Towns with Avenues of Oak,
> Enclose whole Downs in Walls, 'tis all a joke!
> Inexorable Death shall level all,
> And Trees, and Stones, and Farms, and Farmer fall.[4]

Finally, Pope had some of the older tourist equipment. He was more of an antiquarian than has generally been recognised; and, to take a single example, *Windsor-Forest* embodies a sustained allusion to patriotic 'meeting of the waters' themes set out in Camden, Spenser, Drayton and Milton.[5] Lacking only good health and freedom from family ties, Pope had almost all the proper attributes of an eighteenth-century traveller.

Yet he never quite became such an animal, and the practical disabilities do not account for the whole omission, though they do for some of it. Pope's own preferred term, 'ramble', is indicative here. While the word was by no means idiosyncratic (Prior and Berkeley amongst others use it to describe their journeys), Pope developed a special fondness for *ramble* and often employs it to the exclusion of more likely synonyms. *The Oxford English Dictionary* gives the verb as the basic mode with the noun as a derivative: 'An act of rambling; a walk (formerly any excursion or journey) without definite route or other aim than recreation or pleasure.' Similarly with the verb: 'To wander, travel, make one's way about ... in a free unrestrained manner and without definite aim or direction.' In both cases the first example cited is from the seventeenth century. Now it is immediately clear that Pope's rambles invariably *did* have a definite route, however jagged or irregular owing to changes in plan. It is fair to conclude, I think, that the term as he employs it carries a certain disingenuous quality of freewheeling or spontaneity: it reflects a level of aspiration, something Pope would like to associate with his travels, rather than just the bare reality. And 'recreation [and] pleasure', though no doubt a large part of Pope's aim, can scarcely be called an accurate or full description of his motives; they included elements of self-education, renewal both nervous and physical, compliance with social obligations, and so on. As with most aspects of his life, Pope took his rambling fairly seriously. And as with many other things, he invented a vocabulary for talking about it in jocose or dismissive accents.

Whenever the word appears in his letters (it never figures in his poetry, outside the early imitations of Chaucer), the tone is one of slight disparagement. It is as though Pope wishes to belittle his own sense of enjoyment, or to suggest he ought to be doing something more worthwhile. Sometimes the ramble is seen as interrupting business or social contacts: 'I hope all health will attend you till we meet again which I fear will now not be till after my Rambles in the Country.'[6] It is often an excuse for not writing letters: 'The same cause that commonly occasions all sorts of negligence in our Sex to yours, has hinder'd thus long my answering your most obliging Letter; I mean A Rambling way of Life which I have run into these two months & upwards.'[7] Again, Pope writes to John Caryll of a plan with Lord Jersey 'to have run away to see the Ile of Wight and Stanted. He thought it a mere ramble, but my design lay deeper, to have got to you.'[8] The overtones of the word are interestingly suggested by a letter from London to Sir William Trumbull at Easthampstead, written at the date of *Windsor-Forest*: 'I daily meet here in my Walks with numbers of people who have all their Lives been rambling out of their Nature, into one Business or other, and ought to be sent into Solitude to Study themselves over again.'[9]

Yet all the time it is clear that Pope derived a good deal of sustenance from his journeys, and looked forward to them with keen anticipation. This relish shows through the perpetual complaints about bad roads or constitutional upsets: as in a message to Martha Blount from Stowe in 1739.

Your next direction is to Sir Tho. Lyt. at Hagley near Stowerbridge, Worcestershire, where I hope to be on the Tenth, or Sooner if Mr Lyt: come: Mr Grenville was here & told me he expected him in 2 or

3 days, so I think we may travel on the 8th or 9th tho' I never saw this Place in half the beauty and perfection it now has, I want to leave it to hasten my return towards You, or otherwise I could pass three months in agreable Rambles & slow Journies. I dread that to Worcester & back, for every one tells me tis perpetual Rock, & the worst of rugged roads; which really not only hurt me at present, but leave Consequences very uneasy to me.[10]

Again and again in the later years one comes on similar worries regarding the state of the roads: 'If ever you draw my affections nearer Devonshire than the Bath, you will have cause to think your self very Powerfull; for there's no Journey I dread like it, not even to Rome, tho both the Pope & Pretender are there. The last ten miles of Rock, between Marlborow & Bath almost killed me once, & I really believe the Alps are more passable than from thence to Exeter.'[11] There is nothing here of the mixed horror and excitement with which picturesque travellers negotiate the dizzy route past the cliffs of Penmaenmawr; Pope never makes any pretence to enjoyment where travelling rough is concerned. As he told Ralph Allen, 'the Journies I have now made will disqualify me from making more, till I become almost a New Body ... I am really otherwise Sore & sick of a Journey so many days after it, that it deprives me of all the Enjoyment & Quiet I propose by it & can only give my Friends Pain & no pleasure.'[12] A different kind of hazard from Cotswold stone was provided by Sussex mud, and like every traveller of the time Pope would have understood the comment by Horace Walpole that 'Sussex is a great damper of curiosities'.[13] For Pope, particularly after his coach accident in 1726, the better roads which the turnpike system promised, and which Defoe welcomed so effusively in his *Tour*, came into the category of a necessity rather than a luxury.

Pope's addiction to travel became a byword with his friends. The Duchess of Buckingham wrote urging him to make his peace with his mother 'for staying abroad soe long she will probably describe You by the Gadder as she did Mr [Speaker] Compton by the Prater'. A few years later Swift told the Earl of Oxford, 'I am glad to hear Mr Pope is grown a Rambler; because I hope it will be for his Health.'[14] There was perhaps some covert flattery intended here, because Oxford himself nurtured the same inclinations: 'Mrs caesar tells me I have got such a habit of

Rambling that she supposes I shall be like Teague never stand still.'[15] His journeys of the 1720s and 1730s have been printed from the Portland manuscripts, and they make mildly entertaining reading with some nicely prejudiced remarks on the subject of Palladian architecture. As for Pope, he was of course never to write any finished account of his trips; indeed he wrote nothing quite as self-conscious and elaborate as the description of 'a tedious ramble of six weeks through South and North Wales' (mainly South, in fact) which David Mallet sent to him in August 1734, while he was himself away on a visit to Bevis Mount.[16] Pope's own masterpieces of description relate to single occasions or to a sojourn in one place: notably, those devoted to Stonor (1717), Stanton Harcourt (1718), Sherborne (?1724) and Netley (1734).[17] In most cases the letter in question was not published in Pope's lifetime, as though he wished to avoid a return volley of similar descriptive sketches—understandable for a man whose every moral essay produced half a dozen essays on taste in confirmation or rebuttal.

II

Exactly when 'the Spirit of Rambling', a phrase he used to Allen,[18] descended on Pope it is hard to be certain. His first extended visit was to William Walsh, at Abberley in Worcestershire, during the summer of 1707. This occasioned Trumbull's often-cited remark that the young man had undertaken 'a dreadful long journey'—an indication of his visible frailty—and a strenuously witty letter from Pope to Anthony Englefield.[19] In this he speaks of a 'change of *Air*', again reminding us of the recuperative aim of travel and at the same time hinting at a desire for novelty—something Pope was often forced to suppress, but which emerges in his later years as a flight from *ennui*. One function of the annual jaunt was to take the poet out of himself and to avoid deadening routine (see his comments on Martha Blount in the letter to Hugh Bethel of 25 September 1737). He more than once regretted not being able to take sea-trips, which would allow him to visit Swift in Ireland or Bolingbroke in France. But his chest disorder forbade it, and he was forced to confine himself to more gradual changes of air—such as the temperate champaign districts of southern England could afford him.

After the visit to Abberley, while the young poet was busy establishing himself in London he seems to have strayed very little outside the region between Berkshire and the capital. He went to visit Caryll at Ladyholt in the early summer of 1711, returning to his own 'Hermitage' in May; and the following year spent a matter of two months there. He went down to see Swift in his windy refuge on the Downs near Wantage in July 1714; and the following month made the first of at least a dozen visits to Bath. By this time he was taking regular trips to Oxford, principally in order to consult books for use in his *Iliad* translation, but also to extend his acquaintance with University figures like Dr George Clarke. Oxford lay on the axis of much of his travelling, and could be reached in reasonable comfort if a stop was made at Mapledurham or Whiteknights, both of which lay adjacent to Reading. Despite the proximity of Wimpole to Cambridge, Pope never made anything like the same penetration into the academic life of the sister university, a fact he came to rue when seeking subscribers to the *Odyssey* in 1724. It was a fact that Oxford showed itself 'much forwarder in this affair',[20] and indeed (whether the reason was political, or personal, or what) the same disparity had appeared in the *Iliad* subscription lists—both as regards institutional 'sales' to houses and those to individuals. Pope is a prime case of a writer whose outlook and affinities seem to have been strongly conditioned by geographical accidents. If he had had as good a friend as Allen living near Tunbridge Wells around 1740, he would probably have made that spa rather than Bath his main resort; and had the Earl and Countess of Burlington spent more time at Londesborough he might well have made more than the one visit to York in 1716. Admittedly he found the roads 'terrible', but his friendship with Hugh Bethel and other Yorkshiremen offered a regular inducement to brave the inclement northern air.[21] And though he told Swift that they were the only two among their circle 'qualify'd for the Mountains of Wales',[22] the most he attempted was what must have been a very short trip across the Bristol Channel in 1743. His habitual ports of call changed over the years, but the area of operation was always the same. Friendships burgeoned and fell away, loyalties developed and cracked, suspicions arose and were allayed, literary politics took one turn or another, and Pope's gardening consultancies required his presence here or there—none the less, year after year Pope took coach along the same highroads and traversed the same prosperous shires. The Whigs in time were to acquire their Dukeries: Pope had earlier rambled through the earldom of the Thames Valley.

The houses where he stayed can be roughly divided into three. First, there were family homes, those belonging to lesser Catholic gentry around Berkshire—Binfield, Hall Grove, Mapledurham, Whiteknights. These became less important as Pope established himself and as an older generation died off, but to begin with they were essential bases to which Pope could retreat from London. Second, there were homes of less intimate acquaintances, to which Pope was invited on specific occasions. In this group we could put Holm Lacey in Herefordshire, where Pope seems to have been a guest of Lady Scudamore in 1725 (a trip to the same county in 1717 had been planned but put off). Comparable is Leighs, the Essex home of the Duchess of Buckingham, where Pope was bidden three or four times and where he actually stayed on at least one occasion. In the same county, some way further from the capital, was Gosfield, home of the Knight family; it is not certain that Pope went there, despite legend and odd bits of circumstantial evidence, and despite a promise in 1727. West Wickham in Kent, where the minor poet Gilbert West lived, may also have received a single visit, in the early part of 1743. Several other such houses lay in the ambit of the major itineraries fanning out westwards from Reading, in Oxfordshire, Gloucestershire or Wiltshire. These include Tottenham, belonging to Lord Bruce, Burlington's brother-in-law (1734); Middleton, home of Lord Carleton (1716); Rentcomb, seat of Sir John Guise (1721); and Dodington, belonging to Sir William Codrington (1728).

The most important of these categories is that of Pope's regular stopping points: for the most part substantial houses at the centre of large estates, owned by men of considerable local (if not national) significance. A further subdivision here would mark off 'suburban' from rural seats. Bolingbroke's Dawley was too near Twickenham to be regularly used for sleeping in, though it was of great avail for talking and philosophising. On the other hand Riskins was far enough from London to be the occasion for a minor ramble or to be the last stage of a longer journey. Pope was frequently there in the mid 1720s, though not as often as Lord Bathurst would have desired. Pope certainly knew other great houses just outside London (Chiswick, perhaps Canons, Marble Hill of course), but in such cases he would be paying a call for a limited period during the day. His rambles involved more extended periods as a house-guest, and it was these privileged sojourns around which the rambles were built. Pope was far from indifferent to natural beauty, but his routes were chosen not to maximise spectacle: they were intended to be pleasant and efficacious ways of getting from one centre of civilisation to another.

It is in this light that we should consider the proud announcements of journeys under way or in prospect. Of course there is some vanity displayed—the sickly disadvantaged boy had come a long way, and was not averse to parading his familiarity with the great:

> I have been indispensably obliged to pass some days at almost every house along the Thames; half my acquaintance being upon the breaking up of the Parliament become my neighbours. After some attendance on my Lord Burlington, I have been at the Duke of Shrewsbury's, Duke of Argyle's, Lady Rochester's, Lord Percival's, Mr Stonor's, Lord Winchelsea's, Sir Godfrey Kneller's (who has made me a fine present of a picture) and Dutchess Hamilton's. All these have indispensable claims to me, under penalty of the imputation of direct rudeness, living within 2 hours sail of Chiswick. Then I am obliged to pass some days between my Lord Bathursts, and three or four more on Windsor side. Thence to Mr Dancastle, and my relations on Bagshot Heath. I am also promised three months ago to the Bishop of Rochester for 3 days on the other side of the water ... In a word, the minute I can get to you, I will, tho' Lintot's accounts are yet to settle, and three parts of my year's task to do.[23]

In fact the leading strategy here is to placate Caryll for not having made a promised visit. The same thing happened in other years, and one suspects that Pope was often glad of an excuse not to go to Ladyholt. In the letter cited, from 1717, Pope continues, 'I had forgot to tell you in my list of rambles (which if it goes on at this rate will shortly exceed in dimension the map of the children of

Israel) that I must necessarily go some time this season to my
Lord Harcourt's in Oxfordshire.' It was in this summer that his
rambles became really complicated, so that he had to work out
routes and times of arrival in careful detail. His correspondence
starts to read like an annotated Bradshaw: 'Indeed I have of late
had a smaller share of Health than ever, & in hope of amending
it, I shall ramble about the Kingdom, as you are to do, most part
of the Summer [1734]. I wish it may so happen as we may meet in
our progress. If you go to Down Amney, I go to Ciceter, if you go
to Portsmouth, I shall be at Southampton, if you ramble near
Oxford, I shall be at Stowe: in any of which places I can entertain
you, a day or two. If I can, I will return from Stowe to Oxford,
but this cannot be till July or August.'[24] The trips start to
generate their own paper-work: 'It was a very great Pleasure to
me to hear from you, after a long Intermission ... which partly
my Rambles and intended Rambles occasioned. I put them off
with almost as much difficulty as I might have made them, & at
the Expence of writing Letters in folio to Lord Bathurst about his
Plans. I went only to Southampton, where the Roads are good,
the accomodation good, Friends all the way, & a most agreable
Retreat at the End, with a very valuable Person to crown all the
Satisfaction of it.'[25]

The claims of friendship certainly ranked high among Pope's
inducements. But he went for something more than convivial
small talk. As Horace Walpole kept up acquaintance with people
for their utility as letter-recipients, so Pope seems to have been
drawn to men whose territorial influence and rural vocation
answered his own poetic needs. It has been recently observed of
the *Epistle to Burlington* that 'Pope's concern with houses and
estates expands into a concern with the country, indeed with
civilization, as a whole'.[26] This is not the place to explore what
the country house ideal or the image of the planned garden
meant to Pope: the attitudes that went to make his literary and
private personality have been sensitively described by Maynard
Mack, Howard Erskine-Hill, Peter Dixon and others. I wish to
remark only that Pope's rambles were a way of keeping him in
intimate contact with those places where the art of living was
cultivated in opulent (but rarely ostentatious) surroundings.
Pope could act as environmental designer, could escape from the
cramping limitations of Twickenham, could view antiquities and

local showplaces, and could share in the daily round of those whom he celebrated in poetry. The ramble made actual a familiarity and social inwardness which were otherwise to some degree a fiction.

It was in a handful of great houses that dream and reality could be brought most closely together. There was Cirencester, at least ten times between 1718 and 1743; Stowe, eight or more occasions between 1725 and 1741, with other projected visits prevented by special circumstances; and Prior Park, regular annual visits in the last part of Pope's life. Slightly more intermittent was attendance at Rousham, perhaps five or six times over 15 years. In the same part of the country lay Adderbury, where Pope could rely on 'a little Bed' to be available;[27] Cornbury, an occasional point of call over 25 years; and, further south, Marston. Stanton Harcourt and the adjacent Cockthorpe seem to have dropped from the itinerary after a famous stay in 1718, when Pope made excellent progress with his Homer. By contrast Wimpole and its humbler sister-house Down Hall, on the other side of England, saw little of Pope, despite the longevity of his friendship with the second Earl of Oxford. Where Matthew Prior had been a habitué, Pope came occasionally as a welcome but perhaps stiffly received house-guest.

Outside this region one thinks of Sherborne, which surprisingly in view of his links with the Digby family Pope may only have visited on one longe-heralded occasion.[28] It is possible that the death of Robert Digby in 1726 may have deterred further journeys to Dorset, just as the loss of Simon Harcourt in 1720 may have explained Pope's absence from the Harcourt home. In both cases he kept in touch with an older generation and continued to exercise his literary gifts on behalf of the family, but without an easy friendship between contemporaries the habit of visiting dropped away. And then there is Bevis Mount, not perhaps a great house exactly, but a charming and impressive seat where Pope obviously felt entirely at home—his stay there was generally protracted, and his letters bespeak his delight in the surroundings. In part this may be put down to the character of his host, the Earl of Peterborough, whom Pope admired for his wit, vivacity and magnanimous spirit. A spell at Bevis Mount inevitably meant a special detour, or at least a ramble in itself: Pope often came home through Basingstoke and thence into

Berkshire. Like the topographical writers he liked to make a 'circuit' rather than a straight linear out-and-return journey. It added to the improvisatory quality he sought to give his highly organised rambles.

Towards the end of his life, when he no longer had an aged mother to look after, Pope made more of a ceremony of his rambling. An added ingredient now, carrying with it both pain and pleasure, was supplied by nostalgic reflection. 'In the Summer', he told Swift in 1739, 'I generally ramble for a Month, to Lord Cobham's, the Bath, or elsewhere. In all those Rambles, my Mind is full of the Images of you and poor Gay, with whom I travell'd so delightfully two Summers.'[29] The years in question were 1726 and 1727; Swift had spent a fair amount of time, before and after this date, in wandering over Ireland; while Gay became more willing to carry his plump frame round the countryside to places like Holm Lacey in the late 1720s. Again, Pope writes to Martha Blount of a planned excursion to Mapledurham and Windsor Forest, 'This may be the last time I shall see those Scenes of my past Life, where I have been so happy, & I look upon one of them in particular in this Light, since it was there I first knew you.'[30] The memory of the Forest was never far from Pope's consciousness: 'I often give a Range to my Imagination, & goe a strolling with . . . you, up & down Binfield Wood, or over Bagshot Heath.'[31] His rambles took him to favourite haunts, as well as to new scenes and much-desired spectacles like Netley Abbey. The refreshment he gained need not entail a long journey, provided there was a change of company and atmosphere. The picturesque somehow required a degree of remoteness, but Pope's aesthetic senses sharpened as soon as he was well clear of Hounslow Heath.

In the final years any kind of travel became even more of an effort. Paradoxically, as the quest for health grew more urgent, so the discomforts of each spell away from home increased. In 1740 Pope wrote to the Earl of Orrery of 'having been myself upon a wild Winter Ramble (not unlike a Scythian expedition) for near three months, essaying the Virtue of Waters when they were almost Ice'.[32] As well as Bath and Bristol, he may have tried the spa at Holt, which his physician Dr John Burton had purchased from the Lisle family (themselves commemorated in the Crux Easton poems). It was all to no avail, but Pope clung to his itinerant ways. Less than a year before he died, in September 1743, he embarked on an ambitious round-trip covering Cornbury, Rousham, Oxford, Amesbury and Salisbury. He had not been to the last two before, though Gay had often stayed with the Queensberries in Wiltshire. Unabated in will and curiosity, he submitted only to bodily decay.

Perhaps the most remarkable inland voyager of Pope's day was the antiquarian William Stukeley. His *Itinerarium Curiosum* (1724) begins with a sounding defence of travel in Britain, at a time when 'the genteel and fashionable *tours* of France and Italy' arrogated a young man's attention. In terms that might have appealed to the author of *The New Dunciad*, Stukeley deplored the fact that 'our own country lies like a neglected province'.

> Like untoward children, we look back with contempt upon our own mother. The antient Albion, the valiant Britain, the renowned England, big with all the blessings of indulgent nature ... is postponed to all nations ... And if I have learnt by seeing some places, men and manners, or have any judgment in things, it is not impossible to make a classic journey on this side the streights of Dover.[33]

Pope could not attempt the Grand Tour, and his health made Stukeley's kind of strenuous fact-finding expedition physically impossible, even supposing his temperament had led him that way. But taken together his rambles do merge into something that might fairly be described as 'a classic journey'. Their declared aim was escapist, but in truth they engaged the same imaginative faculties as his own poetry. 'You are much a superior genius to me in rambling', he wrote to the lawyer Fortescue, then on the circuit. 'You, like a Pigeon ... can fly some hundred leagues at a pitch; I, like a poor squirrel, am continually in motion indeed, but it is about a cage of three foot: my little excusions are but like those of a shopkeeper, who walks every day a mile or two before his own door, but minds his business all the while.'[34] We may be glad that Pope, too, 'minded his business' while upon his little excursions. He was never more imaginatively alive than when he was rambling.

Notes

1. A.R. Humphreys, *The Augustan World* (1954), p. 238.
2. For the topographic tradition, see Esther Moir, *The Discovery of Britain* (1964, and my introduction to Daniel Defoe, *A Tour through the Whole Island of Great Britain* (1971), 18–29.
3. *An Eighteenth-Century Correspondence*, ed. Lilian Dickins and Mary Stanton (1910), p. 397.
4. *The Second Epistle of the Second Book of Horace Imitated by Mr. Pope*, 11. 254–63.
5. That he consulted Camden from his travels is evident from references in his letters, e.g. Pope to Oxford, 1 September 1734, Pope *Corr*, III, 430.
6. Pope *Corr*, III, 482.
7. Pope *Corr*, I, 180–1.
8. Pope *Corr.*, I, 411.
9. A. Coyle Lunn, 'A new Pope letter in the Trumbull correspondence', *Review of English Studies*, XXIV (1973), 310–15.
10. Pope *Corr.*, IV, 185.
11. Pope *Corr.*, IV, 156.
12. Pope *Corr.*, IV, 190.
13. Quoted by Moir, *op. cit.*, p. 6.
14. Pope *Corr.*, II, 303; III, 429. See also Bolingbroke's report of Pope's travels, III, 413.
15. Pope *Corr.*, II, 315.
16. Pope *Corr.*, III, 421–3.
17. Pope *Corr.*, I, 429–30; I, 505–7; II, 236–40; G.S. Rousseau, 'A new Pope letter', *Philological Quarterly*, XLV (1966), 439–48. For comments on the Stanton Harcourt letter, see my *Introduction to Pope* London, (1976), pp. 146–9. For the Sherborne letter, see Howard Erskine-Hill, *The Social Milieu of Alexander Pope* (London, 1975), pp. 287–90.
18. Pope *Corr.*, IV, 347.
19. George Sherburn, 'Letters of Pope', *Review of English Studies*, IX (1958), 388–406.
20. Pope *Corr.*, II, 271.
21. Pope *Corr.*, III, 61. For the Yorkshire connection, see 'The Burlington Circle in the Provinces', *Durham University Journal*, LXVII (1975), 219–26.
22. Pope *Corr.*, II, 395.
23. Pope *Corr.*, I, 417–18.
24. Pope *Corr.*, III, 408.
25. Pope *Corr.*, IV, 39.
26. Erskine-Hill, p. 304.
27. Pope *Corr.*, IV, 189.
28. Likewise there is evidence only of one visit to Hagley (*Corr.*, IV, 185), a residence much more familiar to James Thomson.
29. Pope *Corr.*, IV, 179: cf. II, 388.
30. Rousseau, p. 418.
31. Pope *Corr.*, I, 393.
32. Pope *Corr.*, IV, 231.

33. William Stukeley, *Itinerarium Curiosum* (2nd edn, 1770), I, 3. This opening
     journey is dedicated to Maurice Johnson, the antiquarian friend of Gay,
     who introduced Pope to the Gentlemen's Society of Spalding (admission
     was on 31 October 1728). A colleague and fellow-traveller of Stukeley was
     Roger Gale, who subscribed to Pope's edition of Shakespeare in 1725. It is
     exceedingly probable that that Pope was familiar with *Itinerarium Curiosum*,
     but I have not been able to establish this positively.
34. Pope *Corr.*, II, 521. For useful comments on Pope's rambles as a young
     man, see George Sherburn, *The Early Career of Alexander Pope* (Oxford,
     1934), pp. 210-14.

5

WIT, LOVE, AND SIN

Pope's *Court Ballad* Reconsidered

On 31 January 1717 Mrs Rebecca Burleigh advertised the first appearance in print of a work entitled *The Court Ballad. By Mr. Pope. To the Tune of, To all you Ladies now at Land, &c.* The fullest description of this poem has been given by Norman Ault in his *New Light on Pope*, and much of the information he presented was reproduced in what is now the standard text, that is the volume of *Minor Poems* in the Twickenham Edition begun by Ault and completed by John Butt.[1] The bibliographical history has been fully explored in these sources, and in the catalogues of R.H. Griffith and D.F. Foxon. It is enough to note here that a reimpression of the first edition, with a new imprint naming 'A. Smith' as publisher, was advertised within a matter of days; that the ballad came out yet again in a miscellaneous collection published on 21 February, almost certainly by Edmund Curll; and that it made several unauthorised appearances in Pope's lifetime.[2]

Ault gives a general summary as follows:

Now *The Court Ballad* is by way of being famous, and whether it is known by that name, or by Curll's later title for it, 'The Challenge', the piece has been so long and universally taken to be Pope's that everybody regards it as authentic beyond all question. Nevertheless it is only by attribution which in the last resort depends on a statement by Curll. Pope himself never acknowledged it by word or deed, and the only two contemporary manuscripts of it on record are anonymous. Warburton, Pope's official editor, who must have known the poem, omits it without comment in his editions of *The Works*, and it was left to Warton to include it in the canon, eighty years after it was written—which he did without citing its source or his reasons. In these respects Warton has been followed by all subsequent editors of Pope, except Elwin and Courthope, who did at

56

least attempt to name the source, albeit in a footnote whose eight and a half lines contain four mis-statements of fact. It thus comes about that scholars have been misled into accepting Pope's authorship of *The Court Ballad* as definitely established . . .[3]

Ault's principal aim was to clinch the attribution to Pope, which he performed with considerable success. A subsidiary function of his essay is to link the ballad with other shorter items which Ault wished to assign to Pope, and indirectly to clarify the circumstances of publication from 1717 onwards.

Though it fulfils its own chief purposes, this discussion leaves many other questions wide open, and none of these omissions was remedied in the Twickenham *Minor Poems*. Indeed, the latter actually leaves out some of the helpful explanatory information contained in Ault's original essay. The result is that the text of the ballad remains very imperfectly edited, and little has been done in the way of explaining allusions and verbal effects. The occasion of the poem has not been adequately investigated, and it is an astonishing fact that the Twickenham apparatus never once mentions the central figure or episode underlying the poem. Ault's essay was called 'Pope and Argyle', and indeed matters affecting the second Duke of Argyll provide the basis for the entire composition. A recent biography of Argyll makes no reference to the work,[4] and it is evident that the ballad, whether or not we assent to the judgment which declares it to be 'by way of being famous', is seldom allotted to its proper place in history. That is not surprising, for no one has troubled to examine the internal evidence closely enough to reveal the drift, tone and imaginative implications of the poem. In this chapter I shall try to remedy that situation.

I

The circumstances bodied forth in *The Court Ballad* relate to 'three crises' identified by Ragnhild Hatton, which attended the early years of the Hanoverian regime.[5] The first was the 1715 rising, and in particular its diplomatic aftermath, which hover above the actual words of the text but set the scene for its poetic activity. The second is a ministerial crisis which lies at the very heart of the work. The third is a quarrel in the royal family, only beginning to emerge in early 1717 but in full swing by the summer of that year. This quarrel centred on the relations of the King with the Prince and Princess of Wales, and it is crucial to realise that a constant hum of allusion is kept up to the Prince and his circle. Nor is the method especially oblique at all points: the title names the court, and through various modes of innuendo—some of them conspicuously indecent—Pope drives home the very particular application of his wit.

Ault suggests that Mrs Burleigh was acting as a front for Curll, and whilst she was quite capable of her own independent assaults on respectability, this seems to be well founded in the present case. 'A. Smith' who is stated to have published the second 'edition' is transparently a *nom de guerre*, whilst 'J. Harris near St James's Bagnio', who was responsible for the miscellany later in February, can scarcely be anything else. The question immediately arises as to whether Pope leaked the poem to the disreputable sections of the trade, clustered around Curll. He would not have been able to publish such an item openly for a long time to come, certainly not during the prolonged bad relations between the King and the Prince, and probably not with any degree of safety even into the Prince's subsequent reign as George II.

Ault was right to dismiss the suggestion that the ballad had been inspired by a gift sent to John Gay by three of the princess's maids of honour (named in the first stanza of the poem) in return for the pleasure they had received from the farce *Three Hours After Marriage*, first performed on 16 January 1717. As he stated, 'the occasion of *The Court Ballad* ... must be looked for elsewhere'.[6] However, Ault's alternative explanation is sidetracked by his desire to connect the ballad with certain *Epigrams, Occasion'd by an Invitation to Court*, also published in the Harris miscellany of 21 February. The tame and inadquate conclusion, not stated in these terms, must be that the 'occasion' of the ballad was an invitation to court by the three maids of honour, and the reasons for its refusal. Ault rightly saw that Argyll was the key to the situation, but he did not explore either the political background or the verbal texture of the poem with any sort of thoroughness. In order to make sense of the ballad we need to extend Ault's investigation in these two directions.

Central to all means and ends in the ballad is the ministerial crisis which had become acute in the autumn of 1716. The secretary of state for the northern department, Viscount Townshend, was increasingly at odds with the King and with leading colleagues, including his opposite number for the southern department, James Stanhope, and the Lord Privy Seal, the Earl of Sunderland. The arguments concerned the Great Northern War, the degree of support to be given to Hanoverian military and diplomatic ambitions, and the balance of power in the wake of James Edward Stuart's rising a year before. Over the course of the next few months this quarrel continued to simmer: Townshend was finally dismissed on 12 December, and things grew steadily worse in the New Year. It was not until April 1717 that a full-scale split in the Whigs occurred, partly owing to interventions by the Prince of Wales, which saw Townshend and Walpole going into a kind of opposition. A subsidiary consequence of the split was the appointment of Joseph Addison as secretary for the southern department, a post for which he was little equipped even without the bad health which increasingly dogged him in the last phase of his life.

The disputes among the ministry involved some questions of personal ambition, but were fundamentally caused by divisions over foreign policy. It did not altogether help that the King was in Hanover from late July 1716 to January 1717: when anyone visited him there, as Stanhope did in the autumn, suspicions grew at home, and on the other side the King may have harboured fears as to the activities of the Prince, whom he had left in London. It was on the King's return on 18 January that some of these suppressed anxieties came to the surface. As Ault recognised, line 51 looks forward to the King's 'landing' as imminent, and this supplies a *terminus ad quem* for composition. The date is significant, for it is a highly topical poem, up to the day and the week if not to the minute. The third stanza suggests that Townshend has already been dismissed, though the 'ado' over his position in the ministry started some weeks earlier than that event. All the signs thus far point to the fact that composition took place only shortly before publication, most likely well into the New Year of 1717.

But there was another occurrence still more directly relevant to the poem. It is thus described by Professor Hatton:

On one point ... the prince of Wales had cause for resentment: just
before his departure for Hanover [in July 1716], the King forced the
dismissal of Argyll as the prince's groom of the stole. Argyll had lost
favour with the ministry after his dilatory campaign in Scotland. ...
Argyll's annoyance at being passed over [for the post of commander-
in-chief] was such that George I's ministers took alarm ... Unless
Argyll was dismissed, Townshend and Walpole argued, he might
intrigue against them, backed by the prince, once the king was in his
electorate. George had therefore to take responsibility for Argyll's
dismissal and ... he resorted to threats to quieten the prince's
protests at losing a servant to whom he was devoted ... This threat
brought Georg August to heel.[7]

Here we have a vital background to the ballad. It happens that
the start of Pope's long-standing friendship with Argyll can be
dated to just this period: the earliest reference to it is found in a
letter probably written in December 1716, where Pope tells
Martha Blount of dining at the home of the Duke.[8] His
companion at dinner was 'Jacky' Campbell, the Duke's cousin
and much later fourth Duke. In 1720 the younger Campbell was
to marry Mary Bellenden, one of the maids of honour addressed
in the ballad. Ault reports a number of material facts in this
connection, but astonishingly makes no reference to Argyll's
dismissal, or to his position in the political drama of the
moment—the very things which provide the springboard for the
ballad. Nor does the Twickenham edition.

The essential history behind the poem, then, may be
summarised as follows. As the ministry drifted into more and
more disunity over foreign policy in the wake of the Jacobite
rising, a power struggle began between Townshend and Walpole
on one side, and Sunderland and Stanhope on the other, with the
King trying at first to reconcile the parties. Sunderland, who had
been pointedly excluded from the list of lords justices on the
King's accession, and sent out as lord lieutenant of Ireland, now
relished his opportunity to force Townshend's dismissal. Indeed
he suggested that Townshend should himself now be appointed
lord lieutenant, and when George arrived back in England in
January this duly occurred, though not until Townshend had
been assured that he need not actually go to Ireland. (At first he
had been reluctant to accept the post, when Stanhope's letter
from Hanover had informed him of his dismissal as secretary of

state.) It was certainly a reverse for Townshend, and a victory for Sunderland. Meanwhile Argyll remained an embarrassment, a possible focus for discontent in Scotland, and a likely coadjutor with the Prince should disaffection spring up again in that quarter. Sunderland even alleged that Townshend and Walpole had entered into engagements with the Prince and Argyll against the King's authority.

So matters stood at the beginning of 1717 when George came back from Hanover. Later that year, the split among the Whigs was to grow more open and intense; the Prince conspicuously attached himself to the ousted Townshend-Walpole coalition, and in October, after the birth of a son, came into direct conflict with the King for the first time. So began a phase in domestic politics which was to last until the time of the South Sea Bubble, the death of Sunderland and Stanhope, and the triumph of Walpole. None of these things could have been precisely foreseen by Pope, but his poem reflects in its sportive and seemingly offhand manner many of the tensions at court.

II

The ballad consists of eight six-line stanzas, followed by a refrain. It runs to an air which had become one of the most famous of any in use, after its association with the celebrated 'Noble Seaman's Complaint to the Ladies at Land' (1664), written by the Earl of Dorset. As Claude M. Simpson pointed out, 'the chief vogue of the song came in the eighteenth century'. It was commonly found in topical anthologies, and sometimes bore the alternative name 'To you, Dear Ormond', deriving from a parodic version satirising the Jacobite general. Simpson lists many contemporary examples using the air and several more could be added.[9]

To facilitate detailed commentary on the poem, I have divided the text into two equal halves, although no important break occurs internally. The text is that of the Twickenham edition, which is itself based on Pope's autograph with selective emendations from the early printed versions.

To one fair Lady out of court
    And two fair Ladies in
Who think the Turk and Pope a sport
    And Wit and Love no Sin,
Come these soft lines, with nothing stiff in   5
To B---n L---ll and G---n
    With a fa.

What passes in the dark third row
    And what behind the Scene,
Couches and crippled Chairs I know,   10
    And Garrets hung with green;
I know the Swing of sinful Hack,
Where many a Damsel cries oh lack.
    With a fa.

When why to court should I repair   15
    Where's such ado with Townshend.
To hear each mortal stamp and swear
    And ev'ry speech in Z--nds end,
To hear 'em rail at honest Sunderland
And rashly blame the realm of Blunderland.   20
    With a fa.

Alas, like Schutz I cannot pun
    Like C--n court the Germans
Tell P---g how slim she's grown
    Like M---s run to sermons,   25
To court ambitious men may roam,
But I and M---o' stay at home.
    With a fa.

The first stanza immediately gives rise to puzzles and points for elucidation. *TE* identifies two of the three ladies: Miss Bellenden and Mary Lepell, later married to John Lord Hervey. There were two Bellenden sisters, but for a number of reasons Mary is the more likely candidate. (These include the Campbell connection, and a greater intimacy with Pope—another reason will appear in due course.) As for the third lady, *TE* states 'Of Miss Griffin nothing is known.' In fact this was Anne Griffith, another of the ladies of honour to the Princess. In 1718 she married William Harrington, later first Earl of Harrington, but as early as 18 December 1719 she was to die in childbirth.[10] A subsidiary problem arises, ignored by *TE*: why is one of the ladies 'out of court', presumably banished or rusticated in some way? I do not know the answer, but one possibility would be that Mary Bellenden had lost favour in the royal household owing to Argyll's dismissal. We shall return to this issue presently. *OED* gives a figurative sense 'out of court' meaning 'having no claim to consideration', but this seems to have developed too recently to supply a likely quibble here. As regards 'the Turk', *TE* rightly cites Curll's later note 'Ulric, the little Turk'; this was the king's dwarf, Christian Ulrich Jorry, a skilled entertainer. Strangely, however, *TE* fails to take over Ault's highly pertinent observation that the expression 'the Turk and Pope' parodies a prayer which Sternhold and Hopkins placed at the end of the metrical psalms:

> Preserve us Lord, by thy dear word,
> From Turk and Pope defend us, Lord.[11]

The primary joke thus derives from a sort of litany, and sets a note of casual near-blasphemy which is to recur. Since Turkey was itself involved in the current continental struggle, and the papal states were caught up in the diplomatic bargaining, there might just be a submerged allusion to power politics. More certain is the *double entendre* in 'nothing Stiff in', a form of sexual innuendo which Pope most favoured when writing, in pretence or reality, to women.

Of the second stanza, *TE* remarks: 'Though the full meaning of this stanza is obscure, there is seemingly some allusion to dalliance at the theatre (in the dark third row of the boxes, and in the green room) and in hackney coaches.' This is quite apt, though the general drift may not be as obscure as is indicated. It is a world not very remote from that of a letter supposedly by a maid of honour which Pope printed in 1737 and is assigned by George Sherburn to '[1716]'. As Sherburn remarks, the letter pictures behaviour 'offstage' at court, and so does the poem.[12] An even closer parallel occurs in a letter to the Blount sisters which Pope dated 13 September 1717: this describes a meeting with the Prince 'with all his Ladies (tho few or none of his Lords)'. The tedious life of a lady at court is humorously evoked, with references to riding 'on borrowed Hacks' and lonely midnight walks. It is notable that 'Mrs Bellendine & Mrs Lepell' are the first two maids of honour specified by name, whilst later in the original version of the letter (suppressed in the printed version) he spoke also of Miss Griffith.[13]

Some of the expressions used in this stanza can be explicated by reference to *OED*, where the first example of 'green room' in the theatrical sense is from Colley Cibber in 1701: 'I do know London pretty well, and the Side-box, Sir, and behind the Scenes; ay, and the Green-Room, and all the Girls and Women-Actresses there'—an appropriately sexual colouring. 'Hack' probably refers to a coach, although the subsidiary sense of 'prostitute' darkens the usage. 'Swing' suggests the jolting motion of a carriage, but equivocally also copulation: other contemporary senses like 'inclination, tendency' may not be far away. 'Cripple Chairs' cannot be found in *OED*: it calls up an image of gouty peers and dissolutes in the mould of Old Q. 'Oh lack' is a corruption of 'alack', which *OED* terms an exclamation 'of dissatisfaction, reprobation, or deprecation', citing Skeat's proposed etymology for a word meaning 'reproach, disgrace, shame'. The sexual import in this context is overwhelmingly the strongest.

TE supplies three accurate but unduly limited notes to the third stanza. For line 16, there is mention of Townshend's dismissal on 12 December: a significant touch, but one which needs to be connected with the later part of the stanza. For 'Blunderland' in line 20, *TE* cites earlier editions which carry the gloss 'Ireland'. Alas for good race relations, one must confess that this was a known usage, and connected with the supposed Hibernian stupidity which was marked by a growing number of 'Irish' bulls and jokes. 'They laught at such an *Irish* Blunder', wrote Swift a few years later during the Drapier's affair.[14] On line 19, *TE* comments that Sunderland had helped to turn Townshend out of office. This is of course true: what it omits is Sunderland's proposal, evidently common knowledge a week or two before its implementation, to treat Townshend in ways prefiguring Belloc's Lord Lundy and to remove him from the centre of power. The stamping and swearing bear a direct resemblance to the huffing and puffing which went on at court in the King's absence. Attempts were being made to rally support and lobby clients: Walpole's notorious plain-speaking may be hinted at in the imprecations of lines 18-19.

In the next stanza, *TE* suggests that 'Schutz' may be either Augustus Schütz, equerry to the Prince of Wales, or to a lady of his family. It could conceivably be Augustus Schütz, son of a former Hanoverian envoy to London, and later on master of the robes to Georg August when he became king. But the context suggests a woman is meant, and a relative of this Augustus, known as Mademoiselle Schütz, seems likelier.[15] Lady Cowper described her as too 'assuming' to be popular at court, and as 'impertinent', attributes which might go with a fondness for punning. The ladies who follow are identified in *TE* as Mrs Clayton (subsequently Lady Sundon), who was thought to have achieved considerable influence over the Princess of Wales; 'Lady Bucquenbourg', an extra Lady of the Bedchamber who had formerly served the Electress Sophia (her name in Pope's text reflects one of the alternative spellings Pickenburg); and the notoriously prudish Miss Meadows, celebrated for her 'woeful face' and 'serious thoughts on the state of virginity'.[16] An opposite story concerning Lady Buckenburg testifies to her (allegedly Germanic) fondness for sticking out her bosom as a sign of stateliness.[17] The trust with which she was regarded is shown by the fact that she acted as governess to the children of the Prince and Princess after their banishment from St James's in November 1717. As for Marlborough, the reference is clearly as *TE* indicates, to the Duke's paralytic stroke. Actually he had two during the course of 1716: the second, on 10 November, is perhaps more directly in question as responsible for his final retreat from society.[18]

III

Thus the scene is set, and in the second half of the poem the tone shifts to a more personal, cheeky and familiar note.

> In truth by what I can discern
> > Of Courtiers from you Three   30
> Some Wit you have and more may learn,
> > From Court than Gay or me,
> Perhaps in time you'll leave High Diet

And Sup with us on Mirth or Quiet,
            With a fa.   35

In Leister fields, in house full nigh,
        With door all painted green,
Where Ribbans wave upon the tye,
        (A Milliner's I ween)
There may you meet us, two to three,   40
For Gay can well make two of me.
            With a fa.

But shou'd you catch the Prudish itch,
        And each become a coward,
Bring sometimes with you Lady R---   45
        And sometimes Mistress H---d,
For Virgins, to keep chaste, must go
Abroad with such as are not so.
            With a fa.

And thus fair Maids, my ballad ends,   50
        God send the K. Safe landing,
And make all honest ladies friends
        To Armies that are Standing.
Preserve the Limits of these nations,
And take off Ladies Limitations.   55
            With a fa.

In some respects the fifth stanza is difficult to relate to the
movement of the poem as a whole: it turns the argument more
directly towards the three maids of honour, and suggests more of
a relationship between speaker and listener than has previously
been apparent. Not many individual words call for a gloss. 'Diet'
could mean then, as it can now, either the food one eats or a
special regimen: here the sense is something like 'high living'
(possible punning senses are less plausible than a first ingenious
reading might suggest). The mention of Gay further augments a
sense of intimacy: in the letter to Martha Blount of December
1716, Pope remarks, 'Gay dines daily with the Maids of
honour.'[19]

There are more difficulties in the next stanza. *TE* glosses line
36 with the statement, 'Now Leicester Square, where the Prince
of Wales lived.' But the Prince did not move to Leicester Fields

until after the showdown with his father: first to Savile House, and then from Lady Day 1718 in the adjoining property, Leicester House, which he leased from Lord Gower.[20] An alternative explanation must be sought. The most convenient would be one to link Argyll with the district: unfortunately his London home at this date seems to have been in Bruton Street. Another contact of Pope is needed, and unfortunately has not yet emerged. In line 37, however, there may very plausibly be a reference to the insignia of the Knight of the Thistle, an honour Argyll had acquired in 1704, since this was much the most conspicuous 'green ribband' in Hanoverian Britain. For the word 'tye' *TE* suggests a stuffed pillow, that is *OED*, sense 4, but much more likely is sense 1, 'an ornamental knot or bow of ribbon'—Ault was prone sometimes fancifully to avoid the obvious. I am not quite clear what the joke about the milliner means, although a knot of ribbons would make a suitable sign for a real-life milliner.[21] Pope's descent into archaism with 'I ween' strongly indicates that the surface sense is not to be taken too literally, but I cannot decipher the true intent of the passage. One wonders if some well-known house of assignation may be meant. Line 41, concerning the plump Gay, is adequately covered in *TE*.

In the next stanza, 'the Prudish itch' recalls Pope's 'Answer to Miss Howe', which links Miss Meadows with prudery and then retracts the suggestion.[22] The prime sense of 'itch' was still the contagious skin disease, scabies, but the metaphorical idea of 'a restless propensity to do something; usually spoken contemptuously' (*OED*) is clearly operative here. Again there is a covert impression of sexuality: the phrase might be glossed 'a burning lust for prudery'. At line 45, *TE* supplies the name of Lady Rich, wife of a Field-Marshal. To this can be added the fact that she was formerly Elizabeth Griffith, sister of that Anne who is addressed in the poem.[23] In the next line it is simple to identify Mrs Howard, 'mistress of George II, and friend of Swift'. But the note in *TE* is proleptic: at this stage, Mrs Howard was a woman of the bedchamber to the Princess. The date at which the Prince transferred his affections to Mrs Howard has been inconclusively debated: what is clear from surviving correspondence is that she and her husband were on bad terms, if not actually separated, by about 1720.[24] Pope certainly knew her

by September 1717, for her mentions an interesting conversation
with her at Hampton Court in his letter to the Blount sisters.[25]
But the intimacy she enjoyed with the Scriblerian wit belongs
rather to her years as *maitresse en titre*, a decade or so later. Pope's
language here does not suggest that Mrs Howard's subsequent
reputation for frigidity had yet been acquired.

   So we reach the last stanza, in many ways closer to the feeling
of Dorset's poem than its predecessors. 'Fair maids' applies
specifically to the three court ladies, but its phrasing allows one to
take it almost as the generalised audience whom Dorset had
addressed. At line 51, we have an almost formulaic prayer to
greet the King, who was to land at Margate on 18 January: these
journeys to and from Hanover were by no means always placid
affairs, and a loyal subject could say 'amen' to such a request. But
Pope was scarcely such a loyal subject, and here at the end of his
ballad he is at his most wickedly irreverent. On line 53, *TE* has
the comment, 'A frequent subject of political controversy . . . but
a *double entendre* is evident.' Quite apart from the obscene
implications, there is some complexity in the surface meaning.
There may be a reference to the fear in some quarters that
England would need to maintain a large military force to support
the activities of Hanover in the continental theatre (though
currently that was more a matter of naval support in the Baltic).
Possibly there is a hint that Argyll resented the six thousand
Dutch troops which had been sent him to speed up the
suppression of the Jacobite rising. Argyll remained a hero in
some quarters, despite his replacement by Cadogan, and he had
many supporters among the military hierarchy. The
penultimate line could certainly be read to say, 'Do not let
Hanoverian interests override our own national well-being.' As
to the last line, there seems to be a pun on the sense of limit, 2f, in
OED: 'The prescribed period of repose after child-bearing.' The
Princess had been delivered of a still-born son in November 1716.
After this, it took her some weeks to regain her strength: her
husband meanwhile set off on what has been termed 'a quasi-
royal progress through the southern counties'.[26] It was this bid for
popularity—an attempt, as we might say nowadays, to acquire a
power-base—which prompted the King finally to return from
Hanover.

   To read the poem in this way is to see in the ending a bold

allusion to the current activities of Prince and Princess. Once we have taken this step, it is possible to look back at the ballad as a whole, and see if such implications are not present all along. In the first stanza we encountered a question as to the identity of Miss Bellenden, and the problem as to which lady was 'out of court'. A consideration beyond those I raised *in situ* can now be brought forward. The Prince had made addresses to Mary Bellenden, some time before 1720—the year in which she contracted her secret marriage to Jacky Campbell and left the court. It may be that Mary's rebuff to the Prince, which she later reported to Mrs Howard, had strained relations at court.[27] In the second stanza, 'Garrets hung with green' could refer not to theatrical green-rooms, but to the Green Gallery at Hampton Court where there was a pavilion set aside for cards, and much favoured by the Princess. In the fourth stanza the phrase regarding Mrs Clayton's courting 'the Germans' could refer innocently to the Hanoverian entourage: but it might be a dig at the lady's influence with Caroline herself.[28] There might be a suggestion in the fifth stanza concerning the pretensions to learning which the Princess harboured, and which caused her to patronise men such as Samuel Clarke, whom she set on to his dispute with Leibniz in 1715 and 1716. Neither the Prince nor the Princess figures in Ault's essay, but the ballad makes a much more challenging sense if the royal surroundings of the three ladies are allowed due weight. (Curll, incidentally, entitled the poem 'The Challenge', a choice without obvious propriety.) All these accumulated hints of *lèse-majesté* come together in the final stanza, which is couched in the form of a solemn national ceremony. Twelve years later Pope was to make the coronation of George and Caroline an important component in the imaginative design of *The Dunciad*.

IV

Finally, we may ask if there is any more explicit occasion which would give added point to the poem, and might support the reading I have proposed. I think there is. In January 1717 Argyll's estranged wife died. This meant that the Duke was at last free to marry Jane Warburton, who had been his mistress since 1711. According to Argyll's biographer, she refused to do this until after a proper interval. Thus the marriage did not take place until 6 June following. By that time Jane was already pregnant: her eldest daughter was born in November of that year, with the assistance of the royal physician Sir David Hamilton—fresh from attending the birth of Caroline's latest child on 20 October.[29]

This would be an apt circumstance in any event, but there is a clinching detail. For Jane Warburton was herself a maid of honour to the Princess, having formerly held this post in the suite of Queen Anne. Swift had met her in 1712, and as he tells Vanessa, 'sate an Hour by [her] teaching when she played wrong at Ombre, and I cannot see her Defects. Either my Eyes fail me, or they are partiall.'[30] Pope never mentions her: but could such a devotee of ombre, who attracted the admiration even of the choosy Swift, have escaped his notice? Besides, in the humdrum life of court ladies, so graphically portrayed later in the century by Fanny Burney, there could be no more significant happening in their small world than the forthcoming wedding of a maid to a great duke. That Pope was very well acquainted with the Duke himself is scarcely necessary to the argument.

Here, at last, we have a real occasion for the poem. The Duchess died on 16 January: if the thought can be seriously entertained that Pope would be unaware of the event, it is enough to add that the funeral was held on 19 January at Westminster Abbey. Here we are presented with the critical focus for such a poem: the circumstances would explain the supposed connection with *Three Hours after Marriage* (premiered on the very day of the Duchess's death), and points to the King's return as precisely imminent—that is, within two days. More important, it attaches the poem to the doings of the maids of honour. Jane Warburton could at length acknowledge her liaison with the Duke, and shortly afterwards regularise it: the 'limitation' imposed by her status in the retinue of the Princess would be taken off. Characteristically Pope preserves enough delicacy in his treatment not to jeopardise his friendship with the Duke, but his indirection was such that the applications he seems to have intended were lost for more than two centuries. (It would not be a wonder if Pope felt that he could release the poem only by clandestine means.) His sleight in addressing the three maids of honour has effectively concealed the main allusion to the sexual history of another of the royal train, and this in turn has covered up the political implications relating to Argyll and the Prince.

This reconsideration of the ballad prompts two sorts of conclusion. The first is that the poem is shot through with contemporary references, and contains far more in the way of oblique political references than has been suspected.[31] Its exact standpoint is not easy to determine, but along with mockery of the Prince and Princess, there seems to be some sympathy. More especially, the poem appears to proceed from the Argyll camp, which is in effect the Prince's position. By implication it is closer to Townshend and Walpole than to Sunderland and Stanhope, but this is not an axis along which the poem is crucially balanced. Second, the mode of the poem is more *risqué*, more daring and more verbally inventive than previous accounts have allowed. As we saw with Swift's poem on the Atterbury affair (Chapter 3) we can only understand the political message if we examine the linguistic workings.

These two conclusions can be drawn together into a cohesive view of the poem. It takes advantage of the licence afforded by popular ballad forms, in respect of raciness, personal comment, and demotic urgency. Dorset had written a straightforward appeal to the ladies to be 'kind': the sailors were away on naval duties, and anxious that their loved ones should not be inconstant in their absence. The King remains at home. Pope slyly distorts this theme to fit a situation where the King is about to return from abroad by sea, and worrying about the activities of his son in England. The ballad depicts a power vacuum at the court, together with the political and sexual imbroglio which will confront the King on his return. As in the case of Miss Arabella Fermor, Pope has taken an episode of gossip and intrigue, and with his 'soft lines' made things worse, notably by laying bare the sexual elements of the story. The poem clearly does not exhibit Pope's highest powers: it is too close to the form it has taken over, street ballad, to achieve that. But it does show his wit, his nose for political scandal, and his capacity to make use of well-placed informers—all qualities which his major satires would call to their aid.

Notes

1. Norman Ault, 'Pope and Argyle', *New Light on Pope* (London, 1949), pp. 172-85; *TE*, VI, 180-3.
2. Griffith, *Alexander Pope: A Bibliography* (Austin, Texas, 1922-7), I, 60, items 67-70; Foxon, *English Verse 1701-1750* (Cambridge, I, 614, 908, items P762-3, W578. For Curll's possible involvement, see also Ralph Straus, *The Unspeakable Curll* (London, 1927), p. 246.
3. Ault, p. 179. The reference is to *The Works of Alexander Pope*, ed. W. Elwin, W.J. Courthope (London, 1781-89), IV, 478-81, where the work is entitled 'The Challenge'.
4. Patricia Dickson, *Red John of the Battles* (London, 1973).
5. Ragnhild Hatton, *George I: Elector and King* (London, 1978), pp. 170-210. My bald summary compresses a highly complex series of events, of which Professor Hatton has given the most lucid and searching account. See also Basil Williams, *Stanhope* (Oxford, 1968), pp. 241-6.
6. Ault, p. 179. For the origins of the suggestion countered here by Ault, see John Fuller (ed.), *John Gay: Dramatic Works* (Oxford, 1983), I. 26.
7. Hatton, p. 198.
8. Pope *Corr.*, I, 379. Sherburn misdescribes the relation of the second Duke to the third (actually his brother) and the fourth.
9. Simpson, *The British Broadside Ballad and its Music* (New Brunswick, N.J., 1966), pp. 647-51. Simpson derives the music from a dance tune known as 'Shackley Hay'. I cite the title used in the Stationers' Register: Dorset's poem is widely known today in anthologies under such names as 'A Song, Written at Sea'.
10. Miss Griffith is accurately identified by Elwin and Courthope, IV. 479. For her sister Elizabeth, see below n. 23.
11. *The Whole Book of Psalms, Collected into English Metre* (London, 1721), sig. [G4v].
12. Pope, *Corr*, I, 380-1.
13. Pope *Corr*, I, 427-8. The encounter described takes place at Hampton Court, where the Prince and Princess were then lodged, but this does not significantly affect the issue. Pope's dating may not be reliable.
14. *Swift Poems* I, 353. For a characteristic piece of stupidity by an 'honest Hibernian', see *Guardian* no. 132 (12 August 1713), in *The Guardian*, ed. J.C. Stephens (Lexington, Kentucky, 1982), p. 441.
15. On Augustus and Mademoiselle Schütz, see J.M. Beattie, *The English Court in the Reign of George I* (Cambridge, 1967), pp. 64, 179; 'Lewis Melville', *Lady Suffolk and her Circle* (London, 1924), p. 21 (quoting Lady Cowper's diary); W.H. Wilkins, *Caroline the Illustrious* (London, 1904), pp. 162-3. Mademoiselle Schütz was the niece of Baron von Bernstorff, a leading Hanoverian courtier who had been in Celle service since 1669.
16. See *TE*, VI, 343; Melville, pp. 26-7 (quoting Lord Hervey).
17. Melville, p. 20. Both Peter Quennell, *Caroline of England* (London, 1939), p. 61, and Wilkins, p. 213, refer to the Countess as very stout, but I suspect that the ballad is the common source for this fact, if it is one. For other references see *TE*, VI, 465; *The Letters of John Gay*, ed. C.F. Burgess

(Oxford, 1966), p. 12 (a contact with the Princess's suite at Hanover in 1714). Lady Buckenberg (1673-1743) subscribed to Pope's *Iliad* in 1715.

18. The Marlboroughs were involved in the current political disputes insofar as Cadogan was a protégé of the Duke, and Argyll's supporters regarded him with suspicion. The Duchess promoted the fortunes of Mrs Clayton, as the Duke had helped to advance the career of John Clayton, husband of the bedchamber woman.

19. Pope, *Corr*, I, 379. There is however no reference to any of the Campbell family in Gay's extant letters, which is indicative of the difficulties in penetrating what must have been relatively plain allusions to a contemporary. Gay did contribute one short verse epistle to Mary Bellenden and Mary Lepell (*Letters*, p. 33).

20. Melville, p. 31, gives a different timetable, but seemingly on a misunderstanding of the events. Rate-books do not appear to be extant for the period in Leicester Fields: Hugh Phillips, *Mid-Georgian London* (London, 1964), pp. 288-9, lists residents from the 1730s. Some acquaintances of Pope can be placed in the area at the appropriate date, but none provides a likely address for the 'house full nigh' of the ballad.

21. Surprisingly there is no single example of a 'green ribbon' or similar sign in the comprehensive list by Bryant Littlewhite, *London Signs* (London, 1972). A sign appropriate to milliners such as the Hat and Feathers would cement the link with the Prince of Wales, but none is to be found in the district. It is possible that the green ribbon symbolises the protestant interest against the Stuart cause, and again in the aftermath of the Jacobite Rising this would point to Argyll.

22. *TE*, VI, 201.

23. See *LM Letters*, I, 269; Pope, *Corr*, I, 345. Lady Rich (1690-1773) was the mother of the second wife of Lord Lyttelton, the poet and politician.

24. See Melville, pp. 156-72, who describes the vagaries of the marriage.

25. Pope *Corr*, I, 427. Gay writes to Pope around the date of the ballad, 'I am going tomorrow to *Hampton Court* for a Week', and his editor conjectures that this was to visit Mrs Howard (*Letters*, p. 32). It should be added that Mrs Howard's position of confidence and intimacy with the Campbells is well established in her correspondence from this period. For example, in a letter from 1718 or 1719, another of the maids, Sophia Howe, requests Mrs Howard to pass on a message to the Duke. Letters from the Duke's brother, later the third Earl, carry references to 'cousin Jack', that is Jacky Campbell. See *Letters to and from Henrietta, Countess of Suffolk* [ed. J.W. Croker], (London, 1824), I. 35-48 (in the last letter Archibald Campbell signs himself, fancifully but revealingly, 'your slave').

26. Quennell, p. 65.

27. Melville, pp. 69-70.

28. See Romney Sedgwick, *The House of Commons 1715-1754* (London, 1970), I, 558-9, citing Lady Cowper and others.

29. Dickson, pp. 201-3. This is a popular biography, not always dependable in detail, but containing well-established facts amidst some fanciful embellishments. The crucial dates are recorded in *The Complete Peerage*, s.v. Argyll.

30. Swift *Corr*, I, 308. The Duchess (c. 1683–1767) lived long enough for Johnson and Reynolds to meet her in the mid-century: see Boswell's *Life of Johnson*, ed. G.B. Hill, L.F. Powell (Oxford 1934–50), I, 246.
31. There has been little critical comment on the poem. Robert Halsband briefly refers to satire on the maids of honour: 'In some naughty verse entitled *The Court Ballad,* Alexander Pope had paid equivocal tribute to their virtue—the Maids were presumed to be virgins—and sincere appreciation of their gaiety and high spirits' (*Lord Hervey: Eighteenth-Century Courtier* (Oxford, 1973), p. 39).

6

BLACKS AND POETRY AND POPE

In the early 1970s Mr E.P. Thompson and I independently hit on material relating to the Berkshire Blacks, who were active around 1722–23. This showed that Alexander Pope's brother-in-law, Charles Rackett, and the latter's son Michael were in some way implicated in deer-stealing in Windsor Forest. Charles was taken into custody, whilst Michael seemingly absconded. Mr Thompson planned a full-length book on the episode of history leading to the Waltham Black Act of 1723; I planned merely an article. The result was that I published my findings first, having permitted Mr Thompson to see them in advance of publication. My brief article on the Pope connection appeared in the *Times Literary Supplement* on 31 August 1973, and Mr Thompson's reply on 7 September. Subsequently my wider discussion of the Black Act appeared in the *Historical Journal* during 1974. Mr Thompson's book *Whigs and Hunters* followed in 1975: again he had seen the typescript of my article in advance. *Whigs and Hunters* was published as a paperback in 1977, with some additional material at the end.[1]

The substance of Mr Thompson's *TLS* article was reprinted as an appendix in both editions of *Whigs and Hunters*. It has therefore now reached a wide audience, including a majority of readers who in the nature of things will not have read my own contributions to the debate. Up till now I have refrained from any response to this widely disseminated material. I did so for a number of reasons. First, there is little disagreement betwen Mr Thompson and myself on the facts: his fuller inquiries yielded information I had not come across, but it would not have affected my basic judgments. Our differences lie in the area of interpretation. Second, I had hoped at one time to pursue the Racketts in other archives, notably the Chancery files: a daunting task which both of us had embarked upon, but relinquished in the face of the huge prospective labour that would be involved. As things turned out, my circumstances have not permitted this further research. Third, it seemed to me that the Pope story was a side-skirmish in a larger battle. *Whigs and Hunters* is a provocative book which rightly elicited a great deal of discussion. To isolate for special attention the single episode involving (obliquely) Pope would be to play at pitch and toss in the midst of Thermopylae. It seemed right to allow the dust to settle and the heat to subside. Lastly, I was anxious to see whether any objective mediation might be forthcoming. Mr Thompson had suggested that the questions raised ought to be considered by other Pope scholars. Apart from some correspondence in the *TLS* when the story broke, there has been no real reply to this challenge.[2]

As a result, I have come to the conclusion that some response on my part might now be appropriate. E.P. Thompson has treated me with unfailing courtesy, and I shall attempt to reciprocate. I have learnt much from his book, and whilst we disagree radically on ultimates (with regard to the rights and wrongs of political action), that is beside the point when we come to look for localised truth.[3] The Pope/Rackett episode involves a finite body of agreed facts, and though it leaves room for all kinds of conjecture the common aim of historians must be to narrow down the area of speculation to its irreducible minimum. I confess that my fundamental interest in history is to discover what actually happened, and events fascinate me more than ideology. The lure is the uncovering of what was previously a mystery, not the confirmation of a theory. I would rather that someone discovered the true facts with regard to this episode (whatever its implications for our view of Pope, or of Jacobitism, or of Walpole, or of Whiggery) than that we should go on speculating according to our own prejudices. I cannot pretend to have reached an objective assessment of the matter. However, it may be worth indicating the points at which Mr Thompson's conjectures (for so they confessedly are) are strained, implausible or unnecessary. The aim is not to prove his surmise wrong, something which cannot be attempted in our present state of knowledge. It is to show that very different interpretations of the facts are possible, and that a case which has now been given abundant public exposure should not be regarded as the only—or even perhaps as the most securely based explanation of the events.

I

The background to this episode concerns the introduction of the Black Act and its attendant furore, discussed by Mr Thompson in *Whigs and Hunters*. Long before the issue absorbed the attention of modern historians, the measure known as the 'Waltham Black Act' (9 Geo. I, c. 22) had acquired a lasting notoriety. The Act was extended for five years in 1725 (12 Geo. I, c. 30), amended in 1754 (27 Geo. II, c. 15) and made permanent in 1758 (31 Geo. II, c. 42). Effectively it survived for a century, until Peel took it off the statute book despite opposition from the *Quarterly Review*. Its main provisions were directed against 'wicked and evil-disposed Persons going armed in Disguise, and doing Injuries and Violences to the Persons and Properties of his Majesty's Subjects'. It became a felony without benefit of clergy to go abroad into woods in any form of disguise or with a blackened face. Commission of a specific act of destruction or larceny was not necessary for a prosecution to lie.

Contemporary evidence concerning the episode of the Blacks falls into three categories. First, documents in the Public Record Office, notably the State Papers. These include depositions, eye-witness accounts, memoranda of evidence, recognisances, minutes of the Lord Justices, and other papers, almost all assembled by the key government official, Charles Delafaye. The Treasury archives include a valuable schedule of activities performed by one of the royal keepers. Second, newspapers give full coverage of the prosecution and on one occasion supply a detailed history of the individual Blacks. Third, a highly circumstantial pamphlet of 1723 supplies an excellent narrative of the whole affair, even if it is a slightly establishment-orientated view, and dependent on press reports in many places. This work, *The History of The Blacks of Waltham in Hampshire: and those under the like Denomination in Berkshire*, was very possibly the work of Daniel Defoe, though it has not previously been listed in the 500-odd attributions now regarded as plausible. Defoe was an outstandingly knowledgeable student of crime, and it is certain that he knew of the Blacks (as his *Tour of Great Britain*, indeed, makes clear). But in any case, even if we cautiously treat this witness simply as an anonymous pamphleteer, his testimony makes it possible to supplant the vague and remote deponents—such as Gilbert White—who for long served as the principal source on the Blacks. There is also a second-hand account of the Blacks in Boyer's *Political State*, and some unreliable versions in popular lives of the highwaymen.

From the point of view of criminal historiography, the episode has distinct advantages. The affair was relatively brief: almost everything material happened between the autumn of 1721 and the end of 1723. Second, relatively few individuals were involved, sixty at most, and a high proportion of them are consequently traceable. This is obviously different from a town riot, as in the Sacheverell or Wilkite troubles, when a heterogeneous and unstable body of rioters was quickly lost within the swarming city. Again, the Waltham affair broke at a time of heightened public awareness. It overlapped with the Jacobite plot centring on Bishop Atterbury, and indeed witnesses of the Blacks' depredations had to fight for government attention amidst the flurry of informing, code-unravelling and general panic which attended the Jacobite scare. Moreover, in more orthodox criminal haunts, the great Jonathan Wild was then at the very summit of his power. This is of more interest than it might appear, for one particular reason. The Blacks were extortionists and protection-racketeers—as, in his more genteel and businesslike fashion, was Wild. According to Sir William Blackstone,the Waltham gang modelled themselves on the Robersmen or followers of Robin Hood. In fact, though there was a strong social component in their activities, their *method* was recognisably that of gangsters at large. It is therefore important to note the full provisions of the statute, which concern such matters as sending threatening letters and demanding money with violence. Wild, indeed, took a personal interest in the affair.

The affair blew up first, as indicated around the autumn of 1721, and its main course was run by the end of 1723. In fact the deer-stealers who came to be known as 'Blacks', from the disguise they sometimes adopted, were operating during 1722–3 in two contiguous regions. One group was based in Hampshire, and drew its members chiefly from the Portsmouth area. It was active in the Woolmer Forest district, together with the Forest of Bere, one corner of which forms Waltham Chase itself. Another group surfaced around the same time in Windsor Forest, principally the Easthampstead-Bagshot portion. The first group reached as far north as Farnham, and there may well have been associations between the two areas of operation, although the evidence on this point is inconclusive. The Rackett affair relates to the Windsor Forest sphere of activity.

The aspect of this story which I am seeking to explore is that concerned with Pope himself, especially his relations with Walpole. Mr Thompson makes some intelligent guesses with regard to the fate of various members of the Rackett family, in particular Charles's son Michael. But they are only guesses, and no subsequent research has affected their standing. It is impossible to test these hypotheses, since there is no other body of information which might bear on their plausibility. The case is quite different with Pope himself. We know an immense amount about him, even if it is never quite as much as we should wish. His public and private conduct is well documented, and the documentation is augmented in scope all the time. When speculation extends to his behaviour, consequently, there is more likelihood of reaching a balanced judgment of probabilities.

Mr Thompson's theory is that the case against the Racketts was 'not quashed but held in suspension'. He argues that Walpole may have held this charge over their heads as a hostage for 'the good behaviour of Alexander Pope'. This was useful, because Pope had seemed in early 1723 to be 'moving towards open criticism of the Walpole regime':

> He had given testimony on behalf of his friend Francis Atterbury, the Jacobite Bishop of Rochester, when on trial before the House of Lords; and his correspondence with the imprisoned Bishop was well known. So also was his friendship with Bolingbroke.

While the charge was impending, it is argued, Pope was forced to 'tread very warily'. 'It is my impression', Mr Thompson adds, 'that, for several years, he did.'[4]

In support of this reading of events, Mr Thompson alludes to various passages in Pope's correspondence. One case in point is a letter to Lord Harcourt on 21 June 1723: 'You have done me many & great favours, and I have a vast deal to thank you for.'[5] Mr Thompson thinks this may relate to what he calls 'Pope's "great application" at the end of May 1723' to save his brother-in-law from immediate prosecution. It should be emphasised straight away that the phrase 'great application' comes from a press report and is there used without reference to any individual let alone to Pope himself. The passage in Applebee's *Weekly Journal* reports in a gossipy fashion that 'great application is making to men in power in [Rackett's] favour'. The *application* to Pope of this phrase is Mr Thompson's.[6]

Also cited are a number of passages in the correspondence which show Pope in a sombre mood in the summer of 1723. These contain explicit references to the taxation of Catholics; to 'the ocean of avarice and corruption' in post-South Sea days; to Bolingbroke, Atterbury and Peterborough. What they do not mention is the Blacking episode, at least in any transparant way. Mr Thompson detects a covert allusion: an expression used to Swift around August ('all those I have most lov'd & with whom I have most liv'd, must be banish'd') might 'carry a reference to the Racketts'. In any case, the text comes from a transcript among the Cirencester papers: it might always (we are to suppose) have been doctored. A month or so later, Swift replied. His response at this point reads: 'I have often made the same remark with you of my Infelicity in being so Strongly attached to Traytors (as they call them) and Exiles, and State Criminalls.' This passage was excised when Pope printed the letters, and the source is again a transcript: but, Mr Thompson assures us, a 'more reliable' one.[7]

The conclusion reached, in what is conceded to be 'a matter of speculation', is this: the Blacking affair turned Pope 'decisively' from the pastoral mode, and 'directed him more urgently towards satire'. Of course, the shock was postponed:

> Yet, though evidently working inside him, the satire was delayed expression for several years. It is customary to attribute this to his preoccupation with the work on his Homer. But if we recall the earlier suggestion that—at least until Charles Rackett's death—Pope remained in some way a hostage to Walpole's favour, one may see his predicament in a different way.[8]

Thus does Mr Thompson dispose of the most sustained labour of Pope's life, and explain by a single obscure incident a creative process which Popian scholars have been gestating over many troubled years.

II

Before turning to these arguments in detail, I should like to mention two incidental stages of Mr Thompson's argument. One concerns the insertion of two new lines in *Windsor Forest* on its publication in 1713:

> Fair *Liberty, Britannia's* Goddess rears
> Her cheerful Head, and leads the golden Years.
> (ll. 91-2)

The copy of the poem Pope made in 1712 had four different lines at this point, alluding to the wrongs endured under 'a foreign Master's Rage'—formally, anyway, relating to the treatment of New Forest by William I. These four lines were printed in a note when Pope revised the text for editions from 1736 onwards.[9] It is quite clear that the revised version is more discreet: we should, however, note that this discretion was exercised before the Hanoverian accession, and may well have to do with its offensiveness concerning William III—*not* the future George I. Secondly, Mr Thompson calls the revised a 'more gummy' couplet than the material it replaces. It is also poetically superior, surely; more economical, more apt to the stylistic decorum of the work as a whole, more resonant for the total allegory. The mention of Britannia cements a theme later developed. One phrase introduced ('the golden Years') has often been quoted as a key image,[10] central to the imaginative design of *Windsor Forest*. Such aesthetic concerns plainly occupied a large part of Pope's attention when he revised the manuscript for publication. They do not enter at any point into Mr Thompson's calculations.[11]

A second indicative phase in the argument is this:

> One need not propose that the poet had any active sympathy with Blacking. But one does note that several men who were Black targets or actors in the prosecution of the Blacks turn up as subsequent

targets for Pope's satire; these include Cadogan, Governor Thomas
Pitt, Sir Francis Page and Paxton. Pope kept on friendly terms with
only one of the prosecuting cast, Lord Cobham; but Cobham was
replaced as Governor of Windsor Castle in June 1723, and
throughout the earlier months of the year Colonel Negus, his deputy,
appears to have performed his duties.[12]

Detailed scrutiny of what Mr Thompson terms 'only indirect,
inconclusive evidence' shows it to be less than that. Cadogan was
notoriously unpopular, and it may reasonably be assumed that
Pope shared the general opinion:[13] but the one supposed example
of 'satire' against him in Pope's poetry is highly conjectural.
'Narses' in the *Epistle to Bathurst*, l. 91, has been associated with
Cadogan only because a manuscript reading (never published in
Pope's lifetime, or for long afterwards) points that way. Satire so
impenetrable and casual scarcely constitutes strong evidence of
compulsive hatred. Thomas Pitt is made the object of fun, if he is
made such, as a miser and a cit turned gentleman, not as a
rapacious landlord. The entire portrait of Sir Balaam contains
nothing that could be turned so as to make it directly relevant to
Blacking. And the idea that Pitt is Sir Balaam was first proposed
as late as 1869: F.W. Bateson reached the considered view that
the portrait 'was modelled on Pitt in the first instance and later
generalised'.[14] Other scholars have regarded Sir Balaam as pure
invention—the kind of reading that Mr Thompson stigmatises as
offering 'extravaganzas' rather than 'a shaft of solid information'.
Either way, the good temper of the satire gives no warrant for
discerning concealed ferocity against Pitt in Pope's breast.

As for Judge Page, it is hardly necessary to expatiate upon his
reputation for brutality. Mr Thompson himself remarks, earlier
in his book, that Page 'was already known to contemporaries as
"the hanging judge" and he went down in literary tradition with
a reputation only a little more salubrious than that of Jeffreys'.[15]
So he did: Johnson refers to 'his usual Insolence and Severity' in
the conduct of Savage's trial,[16] whilst Fielding's Man of the Hill
presents him in colours only a little softer.[17] But that very fact
works *against* the supposition that Pope cherished a special and
personal hostility towards him. The *Dunciad* note, again quoted
by Mr Thompson, speaks of the 'hundred miserable examples
during a long life' which bespoke Page's cruelty.[18] Pope said
more graphically what many other said: there is nothing to

indicate a private pique grounded in the Blacking episode.

This is also true of Paxton, but here the evidence is more interesting. Nicholas Paxton was less of a general villain, though his work for Walpole in the 1730s brought him the dislike of writers and journalists whose work he censored. After the fall of Walpole he was accused of exercising corruption by a Secret Committee of Parliament, but when interrogated he remained silent. However, in 1723 the important fact lay elsewhere. Paxton was only Assistant Solicitor to the Treasury, but it was he rather than Anthony Cracherode who supervised much of the day-to-day business of investigation and law-maintenance, as the State Papers reveal. In some respects he acted in the capacity of a Director of Public Prosecutions. He came into special prominence at the time of the Jacobite scares in the aftermath of the 1715 Rising. More than once he was instrumental in measures taken against the high-flying printer Nathaniel Mist. And he gained the lasting enmity of Stuart Sympathisers for the apparent relish with which he conducted the prosecution of Atterbury. He was thought to be the controller of the battery of informers and suborned witnesses whom the government were alleged to employ, and it was suggested he tried to bring in false evidence during the hearings. Another 'martyr' of the period was the Duke of Wharton, whose lines on the subject have been preserved in *The New Foundling Hospital for Wit*:

> And bid his old tool, Delafaye,
> Keep Lynch and Mason in full pay,
> Paxton should teach them what to say.
> For hatching plots, and coining treason,
> Paxton's esteem'd, with mighty reason.[19]

It was the vastly publicised trial of Atterbury, in which Pope took his faltering but altogether visible part, that long established the reputation of men like Paxton. Pope's only surviving references in prose and verse date from the late 1730s: they clearly relate to Paxton as he was operating in the Walpole regime at that later period. It was not until 1739 that Pope thought of giving Paxton a niche in *The Dunciad*, and even this reference was eliminated when the new passage appeared in the 1743 text.[20] Mr Thompson repeats as fact a story that Paxton hired Whig

hooligans to break Pope's windows while he was dining with
Bolingbroke and Bathurst.[21] The tale was retailed much later by
Joseph Warton; it may or may not be true (though there is no
contemporary corroboration), but it serves Mr Thompson in his
desire to read the texts in a more 'literal' way—here *Epilogue to the
Satires*, II, 140–5.

In each case it emerges that Pope's contact with these men was
slight, inconsequential, distant or non-existent. The references
are sometimes dubious, sometimes exceedingly oblique,
sometimes belated, always brief. They can be paralleled in
writers with no involvement in the Blacking episode. They can
always be explained by obvious facts quite outside Mr
Thompson's area of concern—I do not say quite outside the
subject, because there *were* links between the Atterbury affair and
the hue and cry over the Waltham Blacks. But it is important to
keep separate allusions which could just fit the episode and
references that unarguably bear on it.

What, then, of Lord Cobham, about whom Mr Thompson
might have felt more embarrassment than he evidently does? It is
admitted that Pope 'kept on friendly terms' with Cobham; but
this is grossly to understate the case. Pope cultivated the great
man's acquaintance for a number of years; their friendship seems
indeed to have begun just about the time of the Blacks affair, or a
little after. The first mention of a visit to Cobham's home comes
in September 1724: thereafter Pope regularly directed the course
of his rambles towards Stowe, and in the next few years he acted
as a sort of landscape consultant. Long before Cobham had gone
into the opposition to Walpole and become a Patriot leader,
Pope lauded his achievements. In the *Epistle to Burlington*, as
Morris R. Brownell puts it, he 'propagated the fame of Stowe . . .
[as] the epitome of landscape garden design'.[22] Then, three years
later, came the *Epistle to Cobham*, and this of course was set
conspicuously head of the collected 'Epistles' in the *Works*. By this
time Pope had unambiguously identified himself with Cobham's
political stance. He was proud to advertise his connection with
the peer, before and after Cobham's break with Walpole. There
could not be a more open tribute than the reference in the
opening line of *Horace, Epistle II. ii*; or a more adroitly flattering
irony than that in the *Epilogue to the Satires*, II, 130. It is in fact the
precise inverse of the situation obtaining in the cases just

reviewed: the contact was long, eagerly maintained by Pope, and loudly proclaimed.

Mr Thompson would have it that Cobham played little part in Forest affairs during 1723. Some acts he did continue to perform, however, with a significant relation to the Blacking episode. For example, it was on his recommendation that the keeper Baptist Nunn, almost the arch-villain of *Whigs and Hunters*, was appointed as a Porter of Windsor Castle on 25 June.[23] His personal interviews with Cobham went on at least until January 1723; during the summer of 1722 it was Cobham above all who spurred Nunn on to action, which led in due course to the arrest of Charles Rackett and the apparent flight of his son Michael. It also emerges that Cobham had got the ministry to defend Nunn in a suit which was brought against him in 1718; Mr Thompson does not mention this, although he does give us titbits concerning the keeper's earlier career, and speculates on a 'pre-history' to the running battles of 1722-3.[24] If Cobham felt any misgivings over his conduct as Constable of Windsor Castle, he did not make them public. There is even a story that, as an old man, he returned two deer-stealers to their wives (having been implored to do so)—but as dead bodies strung on a cart. Mr Thompson defends the veracity of this 'firm local tradition' against Professor John Cannon in the new edition of *Whigs and Hunters*.[25] If it *is* true, then the argument that Cobham had washed his hands of the campaign against Blacks grows more dubious. If Cobham genuinely was capable of such acts into his last days, this casts doubt on the assertion that he can be used in evidence to show that 'the general run of Pope's values would have been against the courtiers, the fashionable and moneyed settlers in the forest, the judges and prosecutors'.[26] Pope certainly was opposed to many such people, and nothing in my own account of the matter is incompatible with that fact. But that he wished in every way to be associated with Cobham's values, as enshrined at Stowe during the 1720s and 1730s, is scarcely controvertible. If he wished to repudiate Cobham, he assuredly went a peculiar way about it.

Mr Thompson's citation of names places great emphasis on a sprinkling of badly supported references alleged to be 'satiric'. It blithely disregards a volume of conspicuous evidence to show that Cobham—who was by far the most centrally involved in the

Blacking affair, of all those named—received homage and affection from the poet. It conveniently assumes that Cobham repented of his hard line in 1722, though no facts have been brought to support this.

III

I now return to the passages in Pope's correspondence which Mr Thompson quoted. From them he made his own reconstruction of events, and reached the conclusion that Pope found himself impelled to moralise his song as a result of his experiences over the Rackett episode. However, Walpole exercised a continuing hold over him, through Charles Rackett's tactically delayed prosecution, and this satiric urge was held in check until Rackett's death in 1728.

There are things that could be said on the side: that delayed prosecution was generally a sign of difficulty in pressing the charges, rather than a cold-blooded policy of blackmail;[27] or that Pope actually was engaged in translating the *Odyssey* and editing Shakespeare at the relevant dates, which would have been more than sufficient impediment to the creation of major satiric poems. Pope himself regularly testifies to the crushing labour and expense of nervous energy. But let us turn directly to the central issues raised.

First, there is Pope's alleged 'wariness' in the 1720s. One of the precipitating factors in Walpole's suspicious attitude, we are told, was Pope's friendship with Bolingbroke. In fact this only became fully manifest after Bolingbroke was allowed to return from exile: the first surviving letter between the two men dates from February 1724. Their most prolonged and open relations belong to the very years when, as Mr Thompson describes it, Pope had to lie low on account of such embarrassing friendships. Something of the same reasoning applies to Peterborough, admittedly a less embarrassing friend from the point of view of Walpole's surveillance. The first letter here dates from July 1723, though earlier correspondence may well be lost. The fact is that Pope's friendship with both men flourished and expanded at the period in question. The open alliance of both with the Scriblerian Group at the time of Swift's two visits to England—in

1726 and 1727—falls squarely into the years when Rackett is supposed to have been 'on ice'.

Consider now the letter to Harcourt of 21 June 1723. Pope compares the public gratitude Harcourt has incurred by his part in Bolingbroke's restoration with the private gratitude Pope owes him for many favours. Mr Thompson suggests this could refer to efforts going on at this time to stop the prosecution of Rackett. It *could*: but it could just as easily refer to much else. Pope's next sentence is 'But I shall now go near to forget all that is past,'[28] since these previous deeds have been overtopped by Harcourt's present act of nobility, that is, in respect of the pardon to Bolingbroke. The favours that lay in the past might be recent, and if so they could include help over Pope's appearance before the Lords a month earlier or advice given about Buckingham's *Works*.[29] But they could well be more distant, and extend back to the many kindnesses that had been shown during the lifetime of Pope's beloved friend Simon Harcourt (d. 1720), for whom Pope wrote an epitaph warmly expressive of their mutual regard. Lord Harcourt gave the tribute to his son most careful vetting, and Pope must have regarded this as a favour. Again, in 1718 Pope passed a long period as a guest of the family at Stanton Harcourt, where he made considerable progress on the *Iliad*. There are many such memorials to a well-established friendship. Mr Thompson's theory requires us to fix on a single, unsupported 'favour', the presumed intervention in favour of Rackett. Such selective application to a complex body of evidence makes anything possible. We *know* the areas in which Harcourt did assist Pope: the rest is pure surmise.

Next, the letters written in 1723 reflecting Pope's sombre mood. As I have remarked, none actually mentions the affair of the Blacks. The phrase concerning those whom Pope had 'loved ... and lived with' is directly followed by an explanatory sentence, making direct mention of Atterbury's banishment. Pope goes on to say that he fears lest Peterborough, too, may incur this fate. Mr Thompson would like the phrase to carry over also to the Racketts; but there is no evidence to show that the poet ever lived with his relatives, unless the expression is taken to include neighbourly intercourse (the families lived seven miles apart in Pope's youth). As for the allegation that the transcript may have been tampered with: it is true that Pope himself excluded certain portions of the text when he reprinted it, but Curll naturally did not. We must therefore assume that the copy from which Curll printed contained the same tactical omissions as that followed by Sherburn; if the allegation is to be sustained, that is.[30] The tampering theory has no serious palaeographic or bibliographic support. It is required only if we wish to suppose that certain dark thoughts have been surreptitiously excised. Mr Thompson does wish to suppose that.

Swift's reply is dated 20 September. His phrase concerning 'Traytors ... and Exiles, and State Criminalls' has already been quoted. Swift himself, as an exile, was often drawn to such rhetorical conjunctions. The reputed traitors he would have in mind can be determined with fair confidence: Ormonde (whom he much admired), Mar, Bolingbroke and Atterbury. State criminals would include Oxford. There is no reason to suppose that anything is missing in Pope's letter to prompt the reflection from Swift: the reply makes perfectly good sense at this point, with Pope's text just as we have it. Swift had taken a close interest in the Atterbury affair, and refers to it more than once in his work (including *Gulliver's Travels*).[31] Already, as described in Chapter 3, he had composed a bitter verse dialogue, *Upon the Horrid Plot* whose subliminal message might be paraphrased by, 'Walpole and his gang are the real dirty dogs.' More recently still, in January 1723, he had produced a birthday poem for Charles Ford. One passage runs:

> Observe where bloody Townshend stands
> With Informations in his Hands,
> Hear him blaspheme; and Swear, and Rayl,
> Threatening the Pillory and Jayl.[32]

This was before the Blacks became well known, and some months before Rackett's arrest. Again it is evident that the animus is generated by Atterbury's fate.[33] Of course, it is conceivable that what was a public issue for other writers had a special private meaning for Pope; it could be that he writes indecipherable messages to Swift, in which the recipient will decode 'Atterbury' where the personal meaning reserved to the sender is 'Rackett'. But that is surely to invent complexity where none exists.

From such passages Mr Thompson reaches his view that

Pope's malaise in 1723 was occasioned, not by Atterbury or by the troubles over the edition of Buckingham, but by the Rackett episode. He further suggests that Pope's switch to satire has a direct basis in biographic events, indeed specifically in the clash with Walpole over the Blacks. He pleads for a more literal approach to early Hanoverian satire, involving the need for critics to 'review the assumption of hyperbole'.[34] The general conclusion may be sound, but it is not well supported by the localised instance. No doubt some Jacobite rhetoric has some definable relation to actual events and to an actual view of the world. Whether it is best to regard Swift's onslaughts on the Hanoverian court ('Swarms of Bugs and Hanoverians', he writes to Ford) as 'straight' political comment is another matter. Hyperbole, which Mr Thompson seems to think of as something that gets in the way of true personal expression, can often be a major instrument for conveying a vision of the world. Swift's most fantastic 'extravaganzas', that is, contain some of his most heartfelt writing. For the critic to read them as literary fictions, works of creative *invention*, is not to assert or deny anything about the real world outside. It is simply to accept the facts concerning what goes on in literature, and the reasons why certain writers command a special expressive power.

The evidence assembled here indicates a number of things. It shows that the effects attributed by Mr Thompson to Pope's involvement with Blacking can always be explained (and usually more simply explained) by other known causes. It suggests that far more evidence is needed before we can confidently speak of a new wariness in Pope's conduct in the mid 1720s. It shows how much of Mr Thompson's case is built on supposition, guesswork and the neglect of contrary evidence. It illustrates the difficulty of applying 'solid information'[35] to poetry, however solid that information might be, unless we have some concrete evidence of how the poet did or did not receive the appropriate data. All Mr Thompson's theorising is built upon an assumption of how Pope reacted to the Blacking episode—something history does not reveal, so far anyway. My original account of the episode was based on one set of assumptions; Mr Thompson's account rests on a quite different set, but it does not do more than supplant my guesswork with another guesswork, more generous in the latitude it allows to neglect of the established biographic data. It is of course permissible for speculation to go on, when the facts are insufficient to produce any degree of certainty. But it would be grievously wrong to suppose that any of the 'solid information' we now have concerning the Blacks rehearsed so fully in *Whigs and Hunters*, has yet clarified Pope's position. On that issue we are as much in the dark as we were in 1973.

Notes

1. See Pat Rogers, 'A Pope family scandal', *Times Literary Supplement*, 31 August 1973, p. 1005; E.P. Thompson, 'Alexander Pope and the Windsor Blacks; a reply to Pat Rogers', *TLS*, 7 September 1973, pp. 1031-3; Pat Rogers, 'The Waltham Blacks and the Black Act', *Historical Journal* XVII (1974), 465-86; E.P. Thompson, *Whigs and Hunters: The Origins of the Black Act* (Harmondsworth, rev. edn. 1977). All quotations and references are taken from the 1977 Peregrine edition. See also Brian McCrea, 'Fielding's trial of A.P. Esq. and a problematic episode in the life of Pope', *Eighteenth Century Life*, V (1978), 30-7.

2. It should be observed that Howard Erskine-Hill's important book, *The Social Milieu of Alexander Pope* (New Haven and London, 1975), does throw new light on Pope's relations with the Catholic gentry. See especially pp. 42-102, on the Caryll family. However, the Blacks do not figure in this account.

3. There are other matters on which Mr Thompson and I have specific differences: for example, on the relation of the Blacks to professional crime at large. This is a subject I hope to pursue elsewhere: it does not affect the present issue.

4. *TLS*, 7 September 1973, p. 1031: compare *Whigs and Hunters*, p. 287. McCrea, 'Fielding's trial', pp. 31 ff, suggests that a paper by Fielding in 1740 may support the theory of 'silencing', but admits that the case is 'largely inferential'.

5. Pope *Corr*, II, 175.

6. *TLS*, 7 September 1973, p. 1032; Applebee's *Weekly Journal*, 25 May 1723.

7. *Whigs and Hunters*, pp. 292-3: Pope *Corr*, II, 184, 198.

8. *Whigs and Hunters*, pp. 287, 293.

9. See Robert M. Schmitz, *Pope's Windsor Forest 1712: A Study of the Washington University Holograph* (St Louis, 1952), pp. 23-4.

10. In all innocence I have done this myself: see 'Time and space in *Windsor Forest*', *The Art of Alexander Pope*, ed. H. Erskine-Hill and A. Smith (London, 1979), p. 46. But, in case this should appear tainted evidence, compare E.R. Wasserman, *The Subtler Language* (Baltimore, 1959), pp. 165-6.

11. *Whigs and Hunters*, p. 292. For a detailed analysis of the alterations, amply documenting the aesthetic concerns paramount in Pope's mind, see Schmitz, pp. 50-68.

12. *Whigs and Hunters*, p. 291.
13. See *TE*, III. ii, 181, and the passages from Spence cited there. The reference here is in the unpublished 'Master key to Popery', and again it is oblique. The fullest expression of Pope's views comes in a letter of 9 August 1726 (Pope *Corr*, II 386). As Sherburn says, 'Cadogan's attitude towards Atterbury probably prejudiced Pope.'
14   *TE*, III, ii, 118. Since 1951 the weight of scholarly inquiry has tilted our view of Sir Balaam *against* a narrow personal identification, with Pitt or with anyone else. However, Erskine-Hill, pp. 263–5, suggests that Pope's 'artfully ambiguous portraiture' is based as much on Sir John Blunt as on Pitt.
15. *Whigs and Hunters*, p. 211.
16. Samuel Johnson, *Life of Savage*, ed. C. Tracy (Oxford, 1971), p. 34: see also pp. 40–1, where a satire by Savage on Page is quoted.
17. *The History of Tom Jones*, ed. M.C. Battestin (Oxford, 1974), I, 459.
18. Note to *Dunciad* IV, 30 (*TE* V, 343).
19. *The New Foundling Hospital for Wit* (London, 1784), I, 227. For the prosecution of Atterbury, see G.V. Bennett, *The Tory Crisis in Church and State 1688-1730* (Oxford, 1975). 'Mason' was a woman, and a key witness in the trial. For an allegation against Paxton, see *The Parliamentary Diary of Sir Edward Knatchbull 1722-1730*, ed. A.N. Newman (London, 1963), p. 19. For Knatchbull on the Blacks, see p. 21.
20. See Pope *Corr*, IV, 179.
21. *Whigs and Hunters*, p. 213.
22. Morris R. Brownell, *Alexander Pope and the Arts of Georgian England* (Oxford, 1978), pp. 195–207, charts Pope's connections with Stowe: quotation from p. 195.
23. Public Record Office, SP 44/290/21: see also 'The Waltham Blacks and the Black Act', p. 476. Mr Thompson mentions Nunn's later promotions (*Whigs and Hunters*, p. 220), but does not mention that Nunn was a client of Cobham.
24. *Whigs and Hunters*, pp. 64–6.
25. *Whigs and Hunters*, pp. 223, 308–09.
26. *Whigs and Hunters*, p. 291.
27. It was common for charges to be held over from one session to the next, as the authorities struggled to obtain evidence and witnesses: in the end charges were often dropped or a pardon granted. This last seems to have happened with Nathaniel Mist in 1721 (see successive reports in the *Daily Journal*).
28. Pope *Corr*, II, 175.
29. We know that Harcourt did help Pope on both these matters: see Pope *Corr*, II, 146, 156, 159, 161, 171–2. All these references are clearly prior to the Rackett arrest, and it is wholly unnecessary to invent a new antecedent for Pope's letter to Harcourt on 21 June: we already have abundant expressions of gratitude in the earlier letters.
30. See Pope *Corr*, II, 183–6, 198–200. There are no grounds known to me for regarding the transcript among the Bathurst papers as unreliable, or for presuming the Harley transcript of Swift's letter to be either a more or a

less reconstructed text. (For Sherburn's doubts concerning other Harley transcripts at Longleat, see Pope *Corr*, II, 324). It should be added that Sherburn's dating of Pope's letter to Charles Rackett (Pope *Corr*, II, 181) is too conjectural for much weight to be placed on it. It could easily belong to an earlier year.

31. See Edward W. Rosenheim, 'Swift and the Atterbury case', *The Augustan Milieu*, ed. H.K. Miller *et al*, (Oxford, 1970), pp. 174–204.

32. Swift, *Poems*, I, 297–301, 312–13.

33. Later on Swift did come to hear of the Blacks, when Thomas Power (the *agent provocateur* used by the ministry) was awarded an Irish benefice. There is not the faintest sign that Pope had alerted him to a personal interest in the affair. See Swift *Corr*, III, 116. The letter is quoted in *Whigs and Hunters*, p. 221, from Ball's text, which erroneously prints 'Walsh Black' for 'Waltham Black'.

34. *Whigs and Hunters*, pp. 293–4.

35. *Whigs and Hunters*, p. 294. It is curious that Mr Thompson does not consider the later history of Pope's dealings with Walpole, on which quite a lot of 'information' exists. Their relations were at their most affable in the very period when (according to the Thompson theory) Pope should have been in awe of the prime minister, and resentful of his blackmail. They dined together quite regularly from about 1726 (Pope *Corr*, II, 368). Pope's kindest comments, to Fortescue, come in a letter Sherburn originally dated 1725 but later placed in 1728 (Pope *Corr*, II, 294; V, 2). In case Mr Thompson should wonder whether the transcript might have been tampered with, it might be added that the original letter, once in the possession of Samuel Rogers, has now turned up and is deposited in the Library of University College, London. See *Scriblerian*, VIII (1975), 57. For the best account of Pope and Walpole, see Maynard Mack, *The Garden and the City* (Toronto, 1969), esp. pp. 121–3. Finally, it should be remembered that Pope's first openly political anti-court poem was *The Dunciad*, which was written and, I think, published before Charles Rackett died.

7

SATIRE IN DISGUISE:
John Gay's Welcome to Mr Pope

In Chapter 3 we saw Swift's characteristic use of a political situation to supply the basis for his familiar games with language. In Chapter 5 we found Pope mixing sexual and state secrets. Now we turn to his friend John Gay, for a different mode of satiric poetry. Among the minor poems of Gay, the lines on 'Mr. Pope's Welcome from Greece' have been received with some favour. David Nichol Smith included the work, with some omissions, in the *Oxford Book of Eighteenth Century Verse*. Gay's editor, G.C. Faber, thought it 'curious that this "pretty poem" which was thought well of by Gay's circle of friends, was not printed until . . . 1776'.[1] He was echoed in the standard life by William Henry Irving:

> This poem has considerable biographic interest, as it gives a charming picture of the friendships of the two men at that time . . . One wonders why Gay never printed the poem himself. Presumably he felt that it would be of interest only to his friends, and modestly underestimated the poetic quality of these felicitous verses.[2]

I wish to suggest a possible reason for this decision to suppress a poem evidently written in the summer or fall of 1720. The clue occurs at the end of the third stanza:

> Bonfires do blaze, and bones and cleavers ring,
> As at the coming of some mighty king.
> [23-4]

This has evidently been taken as an innocent simile; but in my submission it points to a vein of bold political satire in the poem, directed against the Court itself. To explain the circumstances, we must go back six years prior to the composition of the poem.

When Queen Anne died on 1 August 1714, Gay was on a mission to Hanover with the Earl of Clarendon. He did not return straight away, since he had few prospects in London under the new dynasty. On 13 September Pope asked Parnell, 'Has Gay come over? Shall we see him here [Bath], or when?' But it was on or around 23 September that Pope wrote to Gay himself:

> Welcome to your native Soil; welcome to your Friends! thrice welcome to me! whether return'd in glory, blest with Court-interest, the love and familiarity of the Great, and fill'd with agreeable Hopes; or melancholy with Dejection, contemplative of the changes of Fortune, and doubtful for the future: Whether return'd a triumphant *Whig* or a desponding *Tory*, equally All Hail! equally beloved and welcome to me!

Pope goes on to speak of Gay's 'Voyage', his own absorption in Homer, and such matters, concluding. 'Pardon me if I add a word of advice in the Poetical way. Write something on the King, or Prince, or Princess. On whatsoever foot you may be with the Court, this can do no harm.'[3] Arbuthnot was to give identical advice in a letter to Swift on 19 October.[4] When Gay came to write his own 'Welcome' in 1720, he remembered Pope's friendly greeting; he remembered its political overtones; and he probably remembered the 'voyage' itself.

For, precisely a week before Pope's letter from Bath, the new King and his entourage embarked for London. They were accompanied by a 'Squadron of *English* and *Dutch* Men of War'.[5] The convoy reached England on 18 September, and it looks very much as if John Gay may have been on board. He certainly got back to London within a day or two of his new sovereign. The situation ensured that he took an even keener interest than did most subjects in the arrival of the Hanoverian Elector and his son—the first two Georges. Symbolically, in view of their later dissensions, father and son travelled on separate yachts. The events which followed became familiar to every newspaper reader in the land; but Gay (whether he observed them firsthand or not) had special motives for attending closely.

Briefly, the King's arrival was used as a tableau of the Hanoverian triumph. It was stage-managed as a piece of Whig public relations: heroes were to be rewarded after their period in the wilds, villains to be administered a public rebuke. Gay's strategy in his poem is to identify (absurdly) Pope with the stolid George, and his friends with the incoming party. Although the details do not always square exactly (Pope's 'six years toil' compares with the four years of exile which the new favourites had endured under Harley), the broad identification is easily and quickly established.

Set, for example, alongside the third stanza, describing Pope's return up the Thames, a contemporary account of the King's journey up river:

> Chear up my friend, thy dangers now are o'er;
>   Methinks—nay, sure the rising coasts appear;
> Hark how the guns salute from either shore,
>   As thy trim vessel cuts the *Thames* so fair:
> Shouts answ'ring shouts, from *Kent* and *Essex* roar,
>   And bells break loud thro ev'ry gust of air:
> Bonfires do blaze, and bones and cleavers ring,
> As at the coming of some mighty king.
>
> [17–24]

Now the royal progress, as described by Oldmixon: 'The King and Prince went into a Barge in *Long-Reach*, and arriv'd at *Greenwich* about six o'Clock in the Evening, being saluted by all the Guns on Board all the Ships in the River, and welcom'd by the loud Acclamations of the Multitudes of People that crouded every where the Banks.' At Greenwich Pope is invited by 'the friend of human kind', General Withers, together with Colonel Disney, to 'dine and lie, / And here shall breakfast, and here dine again; / And sup. and breakfast on' (33–5). Whether the poet complies is not absolutely clear. But the King certainly stopped off at Greenwich, where he was greeted by the Duke of Northumberland, Captain of the Life-Guard, and the Lords of the Regency. Having received certain favoured peers in his bedchamber at the Palace, he held next morning (Sunday) his first state levee in the superb apartments there. This brilliant throng of wellwishers finds its parallel in Pope's reception committee.

At this point a small divergence occurs. Pope makes his journey from Greenwich to London by water, unlike the King,

who proceeded by land in a glass coach. However, their welcome
is otherwise similar:

> Oh, what a concourse swarms on yonder key!
>   The sky re-echoes with new shouts of joy:
> By all this show, I ween, 'tis Lord Mayor's day;
>   I hear the voice of trumpet and hautboy:—
> No, now I see them near—oh, these are they
>   Who come in crowds to welcome thee from *Troy*.
> Hail to the bard whom long as lost we mourn'd,
> From siege, from battle, and from storm return'd!
>
> Of goodly dames, and courteous knights, I view
>   The silken petticoat, and broider'd vest;
> Yea Peers, and mighty Dukes, with ribbands blue,
>   (True blue, fair emblem of unstained breast.)
> Others I see, as noble, and more true,
>   By no court-badge distinguish'd from the rest.
>
>   [41–54]

Now the royal entry, as described by John Oldmixon:

> Above two hundred Coaches of the Nobility and Gentry, all with six
> Horses, preceded his Majesty's. When the King came to *St Margaret's
> Hill* in *Southwark*, he was met by the Lord-Mayor, Aldermen,
> Recorder, Sheriffs, and Officers of the City of *London*; in whose
> Name, Sir *Peter King*, Recorder, made a congratulatory Speech . . .
> The Royal Pomp continu'd till his Majesty's Arrival at his Palace at
> *St James's*, and the shining Show was still brighten'd by as fair a Day
> as ever was known in that Season of the Year. The Streets from the
> *Stones End* to *St James's*, as many Miles as they were in length, were
> throng'd with joyful Spectators; the Balconies all along adorn'd with
> Tapestries, and fill'd with the brightest Beauties in *England*, who,
> particularly from *Ludgate* to *Temple-Bar*, made an Appearance
> equally surprizing and charming . . . It was observable, that the
> Duke of *Marleborough's* Coach . . . was attended by great Numbers of
> the Populace, with Shouts of Acclamations from *Greenwich* to *St
> James's*; and that the Earl of *Oxford* was hiss'd in several Places . . .
> There was not the least Disorder committed in that prodigious
> Concourse of People.

And so on. If not a true Lord Mayor's Day, the occasion was
certainly one of municipal junketing along the route of the Lord

Mayor's procession.[6] Oldmixon stresses that the King was greeted not just by the nobility and gentry, but also by 'an infinite Crowd of Persons of all Conditions'.

A high proportion of those named by Gay among Pope's well-wishers must have also witnessed George's arrival, though not all with equal warmth. The first two named are Methuen and '*Wortley*'. Lady Mary was in fact kicking her heels in Nottinghamshire at this moment, lamenting her husband's lack of push: but within three weeks he and Paul Methuen were appointed Commissioners of the Treasury.[7] Also among the first group of court ladies are '*Howard*', who from 1710 to 1713 had been at Hanover and acquired Princess Caroline's favour; and Sophia Howe, daughter of a general who had been Envoy Extraordinary to Hanover from 1705 to 1709.[8] After the maids of honour have been disposed of, however, court favourites are notably absent. The list includes exiles like Bolingbroke and (in a sense) Swift; Jacobites and conspirators like Lansdown and Atterbury; unrepentant Tories such as Harcourt and Harley (Oxford's son).[9] These were exactly the men of whom Oldmixon wrote: 'In Truth, it was thought great Effronterie by modest Persons, that some People had the face to be seen in the Court of a Prince whose Interest they had notoriously oppos'd.'[10] One of the very few stout Hanoverians listed is James Craggs the younger, who had actually taken a letter from the Privy Council to Herrenhausen giving news of the Queen's impending death.

'How lov'd! how honour'd thou!' Gay writes in the last stanza, with a glance at Homer's assumed lack of recognition:

> What from contending cities did he gain;
> And what rewards his grateful country pay?

This must have been meant to reflect back on the unpopular George, who had gained little honour and less love in his adopted country since the pompous arrival described by Oldmixon. A patent irony obtrudes in the reference to the 'grateful country'. The gratitude is real in the case of Pope, deplorably absent for Homer, justifiably missing in the case of the King.

Why should Gay have reverted to this triumphal journey to London in 1720? The answer is to be found in his very first lines:

> Long hast thou, friend! been absent from thy soil,
>   Like patient *Ithacus* at siege of *Troy*;
> I have been witness of thy six years toil,
>   Thy daily labours and thy night's annoy,
> Lost to thy native land, with great turmoil,
>   On the wide sea, oft threat'ning to destroy.
>
> [1-6]

George had found his 'six years toil' in Britain distinctly uphill work. He always hankered after a return to Hanover, and looked on the restrictions placed on him as intolerable: 'He endured England, but Hanover was his real love ... Did the Act of Settlement prevent his leaving England—then that clause of the Act must be repealed!'[11] Once he threatened not to return from Hanover at all. In July 1716 (as we saw in Chapter 5) he escaped for the first time; he did not come back, and then in a bad frame of mind, until the following January. In the meantime there developed 'a welter of intrigue and mounting frustration', with government business almost impossible to transact.[12] Nor was this his final trip. Right through the 1720s he made repeated visits to Hanover, leaving a cumbrous regency system behind him, and it was on such a trip that he died at Osnabrück in 1727. But of all his unpopular jaunts, the most ill-timed was that begun on 15 June 1720, when the South Sea Bubble was at its height; he left from Greenwich, aboard the *Carolina*. Before he returned in November, the nation had passed through a major crisis. As Governor of the South Sea Company, he had at least a titular responsibility for the events now shaking the country, quite apart from the sixty thousand pounds stock he held.[13] Even then he was detained by a storm which caused the royal squadron to return to port. When he did get back to London, though the City put up illuminations, he ignored them and drove straight to St James's through back streets.[14]

In the light of all this, it is scarcely surprising that Gay chose to withhold his poem. Quite apart from lauding Jacobites and attainted men, it went out of its way to parody the King's triumphant entry on his first coming to England. And its opening stanza made open reference to the King as 'absent from [his] soil'. The 'great turmoil' on the wide South Sea was all about, threatening to destroy the national well-being. And where was the King?—in Hanover. Mixed in with the 'felicitous verses' of this 'pretty poem' is a sharp political satire, which readily accounts for its long suppression.

Notes

1. *The Poetical Works of John Gay*, ed. G.C. Faber (1926; rpt. New York, 1969), p. 164. All citations follow this edition. Also see *The Oxford Book of Eighteenth Century Verse* ed. David Nichol Smith, (New York, 1926), pp. 164-8.
2. William Henry Irving, *John Gay Favorite of the Wits* (1940; rpt. New York, 1962), p. 181.
3. Pope *Corr*, 1,235-55. For the exact date, see Sherburn's n. 1 on p. 254.
4. Swift *Corr*, II,137.
5. My account of the King's arrival is based chiefly on John Oldmixon, *The History of England During the Reigns of . . . George I* (London, 1735), pp. 572-3. This was not published for twenty years; but Oldmixon was in London at the time, and drew on other contemporary sources. For another view of the occasion, see Sir James Thornhill's notes, reported in Ronald Paulson, *Hogarth: His Life, Art and Times* (New Haven, Conn, 1971), I,140-1. For the political message carried by Thornhill's ceiling at Greenwich, depicting the King's arrival, see Ragnhild Hatton, *King George I: Elector and King* (London, 1978), pp. 261-2.
6. See Aubrey Williams, *Pope's Dunciad* (London, 1955), pp. 32-3.
7. *LM Letters*, 1,226-30.
8. Lewis Melville, *Lady Suffolk and her Circle* (London, 1924), pp. 4-13. In the original draft this stanza included mention of the 'harmonious Cowper', Caroline's Lady of the Bedchamber: see *Poetical Works*, ed. Faber, p. 669.
9. The younger Harcourt died on 1 July 1720. It looks as if the poem may conceivably have been drafted first before that date, but the evidence is not conclusive.
10. Oldmixon, p. 572.
11. Peter Quennell, *Caroline of England* (London, 1939), p. 52. For the King's visits to Hanover during his reign, see Hatton, pp. 158-63.
12. J.H. Plumb, *The First Four Georges* (London, 1966), p. 51.
13. For George's personal holdings in the Company, see Hatton, pp. 251-3.
14. Carswell, pp. 68-9, 159-60, 189, 204; Oldmixon, pp. 700-3. In his turn George II faced difficulties on the sea voyage and incurred unpopularity as a result of his prolonged visits to Hanover: *Lord Hervey's Memoirs*, ed. Romney Sedgwick (London, 1952), pp. 200-2, 224-6. The fourth line of the poem may be a veiled reference to the King's notoriously troublesome mistresses.

8

MERCHANTS AND MINISTERS:
Peachum, Jonathan Wild, and *The Complete English Tradesman*

Jacob Viner once observed in an essay on Augustan satire that full-blooded attacks on the entire system of society were rare. Instead, 'Persons who possessed or acquired wealth without deserving it were often subjected to satirical treatment, as for instance in Gay's *Beggar's Opera*.' Viner drily added that 'This is sometimes interpreted by modern scholars as evidence that the satirists condemned on moral grounds a social system in which wealth was not distributed according to merit.'[1] It is certainly the case that satire on corrupt individuals does not automatically carry with it, in an eighteenth-century context, any direct leakage on to institutions and social organisms at large. However, it was possible for a writer, when he chose, to implicate wider political or economic concerns in his attack on particular historical figures. *The Beggar's Opera* will itself, I believe, show just such a process of satiric dispersal at work.

It has been generally accepted that the character of Peachum in the play represents a double current of satire, directed against the thief-taker Jonathan Wild and through him the prime minister, Robert Walpole. I wish to suggest that a third level of meaning exists within the figure of Peachum. Many of his lineaments, in fact, are closely modelled upon the portrait of an ideal businessman drawn by Daniel Defoe, a bare year or two before the appearance of Gay's drama. *The Complete English Tradesman* (1725–7) was for long one of Gay's best-known books.[2] Charles Lamb thought it deserved prosecution instead of Mandeville's *Table of the Bees*, 'as of a far more vile and debasing tendency'.[3] It came to be regarded, indeed, as a classic statement of the protestant ethic in practice. If Peachum, then, can be taken as an embodiment of the English tradesman, this lends added force to the critique of public mores which suffuses *The Beggar's*

Opera: and it sharply reinforces the satiric equivalence of Walpole and Wild.

I

The word *business* occurs twelve times in the play. Seven of these usages are found in the first act, before the ostensible hero Macheath so much as enters the scene. Peachum, the really dominant character from start to finish, is responsible for seven of these usages. The word is employed once by his wife, once by his servant Filch, and once by Mrs Trapes, all in conversation with Peachum. The other two occasions are in speeches by Macheath during the second act. Throughout, the dramatic idiom is pervaded by words drawn from trade and commerce. Mrs Peachum speaks of love in terms of 'property' (I, v, 5); she even sings a song (Air V) which compares a wife to 'a guinea in gold . . . Now here, now there, is bought, or is sold,/And is current in every house'. The expression *fortune* turns up repeatedly, often with ironic or ambiguous effect (I, viii, 11, 50, 74; II, iv, 81, 96; II, vii, 11; III, iv, 2). Similar phrases involve *customer, insure, pension, conveyance* (used of theft), *garnish, payment, interest, perquisite, sum, loan, profit, loss, price, fees, expenses, affairs, agents,* and so on. Macheath anticipates the sequel *Polly* at the end when he advises his doting mistresses to 'ship [themselves] off for the *West Indies*' (III, xv, 3), like a hunk of cargo. Persons often become the object of commercial verbs: Mrs Peachum says that she will 'undertake to manage Polly' (I, xi, 12), whilst prentices are sent to the plantations (II, iv, 94) and Lockit and Peachum agree 'to go halves in *Macheath*' (II, x, 2). Almost everyone has a slice of Macheath, however. It is characteristic that the 'bargain' struck relates to his betrayal by the doxier (II, vi, 2).

It is above all in Peachum's speech that this economic colouring is apparent. He refers in the opening lines of the play to his 'honest employment' (I, i, 9), and alludes to the 'profession' of thief-catcher (for example, I, ii, 23). Both words are applied by him to Macheath (I, viii, 25: I, x, 32). The seriousness with which these parasites of crime regard their own activities is brought out in one of the crucial exchanges of the play:

Lockit: In this last affair, brother *Peachum*, we are agreed. You have consented to go halves in *Macheath*.

Peachum: We shall never fall out about an execution—But as to that article, pray how stands our last year's account?

Lockit: If you will run your eye over it, you'll find 'tis fair and clearly stated.

Peachum: This long arrear of the government is very hard upon us! Can it be expected that we should hang our acquaintance for nothing, when our betters will hardly save theirs without being paid for it. Unless the people in employment pay better, I promise them for their future, I shall let other rogues live besides their own.

Lockit: Perhaps, brother, they are afraid these matters may be carried too far. We are treated too by them with contempt, as if our profession were not reputable.

Peachum: In one respect indeed, our employment may be reckoned dishonest, because, like great Statesmen, we encourage those who betray their friends.

(II, x, 1–15)

Lockit breaks in to warn Peachum over his unguarded 'language'; but in fact the method of the entire *Opera* is to make language spill the beans—betray the hidden attitudes and the real drives. So the scene continues:

Peachum: Here's poor *Ned Clincher's* name, I see. Sure, brother *Lockit*, there was a little unfair proceeding in *Ned's* case; for he told me in the condemn'd hold that for value receiv'd you had promis'd him a Session or two longer without molestation.

Lockit: Mr. *Peachum*,—this is the first time my honour was ever call'd in question.

Peachum: Business is at an end—if once we act dishonourably.

Lockit: ... He that attacks my honour, attacks my livelihood.

(II, x, 24–33)

So the two villains come to blows, when Peachum reports the charge that Lockit had 'defrauded' an informer of her money: 'Indeed, indeed, brother we must punctually pay our Spies, or we shall have no Information' (II, x, 37). Scrupulosity over small details goes with a total moral blindness on larger issues.

The robbers are almost as concerned about their reputation, though their motives are less prudential and their tone more puzzled: Matt of the Mint wonders why 'we are not more respected' (III, iv, 23), whereas the 'profession' of gamester is accorded higher status. But even the thieves fall into the trading jargon:

> *Macheath*: Have an eye upon the money-lenders. A *Rouleau*, or two, would prove a pretty sort of an expedition. I hate extortion.
> *Matt of the Mint*: Those *Rouleaus* are very pretty things—I hate your bank bills—there is such a hazard in putting them off.
> *Macheath*: There is a certain man of distinction, who in his time hath nick'd me out of a great deal of the ready. He is in my cash, *Ben*;—I'll point him out to you this evening, and you shall draw upon him for the debt.[4]
>
> (III, iv, 33-9)

Similarly the women of the town:

> *Mrs Trapes*: The hard times oblige me to go very near in my dealing—To be sure, of late years I have been a great sufferer by the Parliament.—Three thousand pounds would hardly make me amends.—The Act for destroying the Mint was a severe cut upon our business—till then, if a customer stept out of the way—we knew where to have her.
>
> (III, vi, 18-22)

She goes on to speak of a 'considerable' loss, of gentlemen who 'deal with [her] customers' and 'very safe sale'. Prostitution is viewed as a retail enterprise:

> *Mrs Trapes*: ... The gentlemen always pay according to their dress, from half a crown to two guineas; and yet those hussies make nothing of bilking of me.—Then, too, allowing for accidents—I have eleven fine customers now down under the Surgeon's hands,—what with fees and other expences, there are great goings out, and no comings-in, and not a farthing to pay for at least a month's clothing.—We run great risques, great risques indeed.
>
> (III, vi, 37-42)

There is a gruesome irony in applying the commercial phrase 'allowing for accidents' to the effects of the pox on a drab's custom; and a rich dramatic comedy when Mrs Trapes envisages herself at the end as a bold merchant venturer. As she admits, 'Tis not youth or beauty that fixes [the] price', and indeed sex is

completely overlaid by financial interests. She does not even
seem aware of the bawdy possibilities of her language (goings-out
and comings-in); we are nearer Moll Flanders' 'governess' than
to Mistress Quickly.

As well as punctuality, there is another businesslike quality on
which Peachum lays great stress. This is diligence. At the start he
gags the evidence against Black Moll, as she is 'very active and
industrious' (I, ii, 4). Similarly he goes through the 'register' of
the gang, looking for signs of energy: 'I hate a lazy rogue, by
whom one can get nothing 'till he is hang'd.' He comes first on
Crook-fingered Jack, and sets out to discover 'how much the
stock owes to his industry' (observe the first noun). The list of
thefts is impressive, 'considering these are only the fruits of his
leisure hours', and speaks well for Jack's 'presence of mind upon
the road'. On the other hand Wat Dreary is 'an irregular dog,
who hath an underhand way of disposing his goods'. Peachum
resolves to give him a little longer 'upon his good behaviour'.
Others are consigned to the gallows; one for wishing to follow his
trade as a tailor, 'which he calls an honest employment'. Tom
Tipple is too drunken; Harry Paddington a poor 'petty-larceny
rascal'. Rather better is Matt of the Mint, 'a promising sturdy
fellow, and diligent in his way; somewhat too bold and hasty, and
may raise good contributions on the publick, if he does not cut
himself short by murder' (I, iii, 2-19). Elsewhere several
characters allude to the 'industry' of one criminal or another.[5]

Another indicative feature is the presence of a carefully
maintained register of the gang. Peachum is attracted to verbs
like 'booking' his thieves (I, ii, 9); Mrs Peachum displays a similar
awareness of the written word, slightly differently applied, when
she advises Filch: 'Since you have nothing better to do, ev'n go to
your book, and learn your catechism' (I, vi, 23). Peachum sees
marriage in terms of 'articles' (I, x, 18), and in another significant
scene with Lockit reverts to the same accountants' jargon:

Lockit: The Coronation account, brother *Peachum*, is of so intricate a
nature that I believe it will never be settled.
Peachum: It consists of a great variety of articles.—It was worth to our
people, in fees of different kinds, above ten instalments.—This is part
of the account, brother, that lies open before us.
Lockit: A lady's tail of rich Brocade—that, I see, is dispos'd of.

Peachum: To Mrs. *Diana Trapes*, the Tally-woman, and she will make
a good hand on't in shoes and slippers, to trick out young ladies,
upon their going into keeping—
Lockit: But I don't see any article of the Jewels.
Peachum: They are so well known that they must be sent
abroad—you'll find them enter'd under the article of Exportation.
As for the Snuff-boxes, Watches, Swords, &c.—I thought it best to
enter them under their several heads.
Lockit: Seven and twenty women's pockets compleat, with the several
things therein contain'd; all seal'd, number'd, and enter'd.

(III, v, 1-16)

Business efficiency could hardly go further. Peachum, with his
systematic habits and schedule of appointments (II, x, 55), is the
stuff of which corporation vice-presidents are made. There is also
a 'blacklist' of the condemned (I, iv, 4).

It is not hard to establish that such methods accurately portray
the real-life Jonathan Wild. Eighteenth-century accounts
regularly emphasise this side of Wild. Thus the *Newgate Calendar*
uses expressions of him such as *punctuality, profession, industrious,
vigilance, endeavours, method, business, plan, mode of proceeding, office,
care and direction,* and so on. We are told that 'Wild accumulated
money so fast, that he considered himself a man of consequence'.
The summing-up in the *Calendar* is relevant: Wild 'possessed
abilities, which, had they been properly cultivated, and directed
into a right course, would have rendered him a respectable and
useful member of society'. Of course, *The Beggar's Opera* pretends
that the thief-taker *has* become accepted into respectable society;
and by aligning Walpole with Wild suggests that the same
ruthless industry and attention to detail explain the minister's
rise. The 'Regulator', as Wild was known, had his political
analogue in the great fixer Walpole.[6]

II

It is noteworthy that Defoe was one of those who condemned the
morality of *The Beggar's Opera*. 'Thieves are set out in so amiable a
light,' he wrote in 1728, 'that it has taught them to value
themselves on their profession'.[7] Yet Lamb made the accusation
that the *Complete English Tradesman* was equally pernicious in its

drift: 'The pompous detail, the studied analysis of every little mean art, every sneaking address, every trick and subterfuge (short of larceny) that is necessary to the tradesman's occupation....'.[8] And that there is a link between Defoe's heavily endorsed code of business practice with Gay's satirical picture of capitalism may be deduced from a casual remark by Lockit:

> Now Peachum, you and I, like honest tradesmen, are to have a fair trial which of us two can overreach the other.
>
> (III, ii, 21)

If we compare the advice Defoe gives with the behaviour of Peachum, Lockit and Mrs Trapes, we shall see that Gay's characters do indeed share some of the Complete Tradesman's qualities, even if they are diverted to criminal ends and exaggerated for rhetorical purposes.

Like all Defoe's work in the 1720s, *The Complete English Tradesman* was written in the aftermath of the South Sea Bubble, to which reference is made, implicitly or explicitly, on almost every page. This is a theme which will reappear in Chapters 9 and 10. (It may be worth remarking that *bubble* in the sense of cheat or deception is found in the *Opera*, Air XXXVI, as well as III, i, 34). The general note of Defoe's manual is cautionary. From the outset he stresses the need for application if 'gain' is to be achieved, and frames his conduct-book along directly economic lines:

> Here he will be *effectually*, we hope, encourag'd ... to begin wisely and prudently, and to avoid all those Rocks which the gay Race of Tradesmen so frequently suffer shipwreck upon; and here he will have a true Plan of his own Prosperity drawn out for him, by which, if it be not his own fault, he may square his Conduct in an unnerring [sic] manner, and fear neither bad Fortune nor bad Friends (vii–viii).

There is a perpetual anxiety lest the trader imperil his good name: 'Besides, for want of judgment of the goods he is to buy, he often runs a hazard of being cheated to a very great degree, and perhaps some time or other a tradesman may be ruin'd by it, or at least ruin his reputation' (8). The fear of being cheated is of course crucial to the logic of the *Opera*: Lockit and Lucy have an entire scene (III, i) on the subject.[9] Macheath, paradoxically, seems less aware of the danger than anyone else, though it is he who suffers most in the play through treachery.

From the very first 'letter', Defoe counsels his reader to pay due heed to the state of his books: 'The tradesman should not be at a loss to keep his books . . . Upon his regular keeping, and fully acquainting himself with his books, depends at least the comfort of his trade, if not the very trade itself' (12). Much later in the text, a special letter is devoted to advice 'On the Tradesman's keeping his Books, and casting up his Shop' (209–25). 'He that delights in his trade will delight in his books' (210), we are told, and Peachum might well say amen to that. More striking still, Defoe refers to the account-books as 'the register of [the tradesman's] estate, the index of his stock' (210). As we have seen, Peachum pores over his 'register'. Two sentences later comes mention of his 'stock'. His only use of the word *estate* comes in the phrase, 'the comfortable estate of widowhood' (I, x, 18). Gay injects irony into the adjective *comfortable*, but it carries pretty well the same meaning as Defoe's deadly solemn *comfort*.

By the fifth letter, Defoe is ready to apply himself undistractedly to 'Diligence and Application in Business', the cardinal virtues towards which his morality is always straining. Again the emphases are on financial success and high personal standing: 'Nothing can give a greater prospect of thriving to a young tradesman, than his own diligence; it fills himself with hope, and gives him credit to all that know him; without application nothing in this world goes forward as it should do' (37). There is an appeal to the scriptures (Solomon, quoted from the Book of Proverbs), and one recalls Mrs Peachum sending young Filch to his 'catechism'. Then comes a passage of deep puritan conviction regarding the young man's calling: 'Trade must not be entered into as a thing of light concern; it is called *business* very properly, for it is a business *for* life, and ought to be follow'd as one of the great businesses *of* life' (40).

Defoe goes on to define the 'duties of life' which comprise labour, employment and trade. Peachum's belief in these things is plain; even the robbers believe that their activities involve a 'duty' (II, ii, 4). Then, oddly, Defoe gives vent to a whole flurry of Newgate imagery to press home his point:

> To follow a trade, and not to love and delight in it, is a slavery, a
> bondage, not a business: the shop is a *Bridewell*, and the warehouse a
> house of correction to the tradesman, if he does not delight in his
> trade; while he is bound, as we say, to keep his shop, he is like the
> galley-slave chain'd down to the oar; he tugs and labours indeed,
> and exerts the utmost of his strength, for fear of the strappado, and
> because he is obliged to do it. (46)

Such fearsome tortures are absent from the world Gay depicts:
the only penalties mentioned are hanging or transportation, and
they are treated with mocking unconcern. Peachum, of course,
has his warehouse (I, vi, 12): but his contacts ensure that he need
never fear entering Newgate as other than a privileged visitor. Of
course, for Macheath, who has omitted to model himself upon
the Complete Tradesman, it is a different matter. The women of
the town must certainly have known the inside of Bridewell, but
Gay leaves most of the squalor out of their lives. The *successful*
criminal need share none of the anxieties which Defoe's reluctant
tradesman endures.

Defoe now passes to a long section, extending over several
chapters, on 'the ruin of tradesman', rhetorically intensified to
'disasters' before many pages are completed. This portion bears
relatively little on the *Opera*, beyond the general desire to avoid
'misfortune'. Until, that is, we reach advice on marriage—or
rather, *against* marriage, certainly at too early an age. Mr and
Mrs Peachum, considering how they can make their daughter's
match with Macheath 'turn to [their] advantage' (I, ix, 10) are
no more prudential than Defoe. Both Defoe and the Peachums
are alive to the necessity 'to keep off scandal', though the former
soon adds to his cautions against a stolen marriage the thought
that it will be 'attended with a heavy expence' (101). The
tradesman is recommended not to trust his affairs to his servants,
but later a section is devoted to the proposition that wives ought
to familiarise themselves with their husband's business. Too
many wives, Defoe argues, would be gentlewomen, and are
therefore unable to take over the family concern if circumstances
require it. Again it is evident that Mrs Peachum has no false
pride of this sort: she is as expert in thievery as her husband,
though she makes one exception, for 'I never meddle in matters of
Death' (I, iv, 8). Defoe similarly observed that 'Some trades,

indeed, are not proper for the women to meddle in' (230).

Another possible occasion of ruin is 'the Tradesman's entering into Partnership in Trade, and the many dangers attending it,' which forms the subject of a further letter (167–78). Defoe cautions the young tradesman that a partner may come to take over the whole business—'there is danger of his slipping into the whole trade, and ... thrusting you at last quite out' (168). More serious is the case where the partner proves to be 'a loose, extravagant fellow' or still worse dishonest—one who 'by his craft and insinuation' works his way into the heart of the business (171). The image of cooperative enterprise is a sombre one ('Who ... would run the venture of a Partner, if it were possible to avoid it?' (175) and comes close to Lockit's vision of partnership:

> *Peachum* then intents to outwit me in this affair, but I'll be even with him.—The dog is leaky in his liquor, so I'll ply him that way, get the secret from him, and turn this affair to my own advantage.—Lions, Wolves, and Vultures don't live together in herds, droves, or flocks.—Of all animals of prey, man is the only sociable one. Every one of us preys upon his neighbour, and yet we herd together.—*Peachum* is my companion, my friend.—According to the custom of the world, indeed, he may quote thousands of Precedents for cheating me.—And I shall I not make use of the privilege of friendship to make him a return?
>
> (III, ii, 1–9)

There follows Air XLIII, to the tune of 'Packington's Pound':

> Thus Gamesters united in friendship are found
> Though they know that their industry all is a cheat;
> They flock to their prey at the Dice-box's sound,
> And join to promote one another's deceit.
>> But if by mishap
>> They fail of a chap,
> To keep in their hands, they each other entrap.
> Like Pikes, lank with hunger, who miss of their ends,
> They bite their companions, and prey on their friends.
>> (III, ii, 10–18)

It is at this point that Lockit resorts to the phrase concerning 'honest tradesmen' which had already been quoted. Defoe uses less vivid language, but his book too shows us partners 'who promote one another's deceit' and 'prey on their friend'. This is apparent from sections titled 'Of Tradesmen ruining one another by Rumour and Scandal'; 'Of the Customary Frauds of Trade'; and 'Of Honesty in Dealing, and of telling unavoidable Trading Lies'. The last of these seems principally designed to avoid the situation where one may be forced to break one's word, and counsels prevarication in the form of 'conditional' promises to pay. The profession of trader, on these terms, seems as far from 'an honest livelihood' as Filch's occupation of prison child-getter (III, iii, 4).

It would be unduly laborious to itemise all the deceptions mentioned by Defoe, which have their echo in the trickery of the *Opera*. It is interesting, however, to compare the dramatic inset which Defoe employs, featuring a lady and a shopkeeper, with the scene between Polly and Lucy (III, viii). Defoe's playlet is intended to show that people rarely speak their mind in a buyer-and-seller situation; his characters are made to say openly what they would normally hide beneath conventional platitudes. Gay gives us the opposite: Polly and Lucy adopt mincingly polite language while in reality scratching one another's eyes out. Again it is revealing to put Defoe's remarks on setting off goods to the best advantage ('for in some goods, if they are not well dress'd, well press'd and packed, the goods are not really shew'd in a true light' (195), alongside the desire of Mrs Trapes to 'put the ladies upon a good foot' (III, vi, 36). It may be a coincidence that Defoe's examples are regularly drawn from the drapery trade—that was where his own experience as a wholesaler lay—but it does chime in suitably with the steady traffic in 'manteaus, velvet scarfs, petticoats' which oils the Newgate economy. Peachum's 'chap in the city' (I, iv, 84) significantly deals in cambric goods—'a sort of fine Linen Cloth brought from *Cambray* in *Flanders*,' according to Nathan Bailey's definition.[10] *Flanders* was a common expression for contraband lace, hence its apposite choice for the name Moll Flanders;[11] and there was undoubtedly a large criminal subculture built around the hosiery and drapery trade. Defoe knew this as well as anyone, but he cautions his tradesmen against rival businessmen, rather than criminals as such. The threat is personal, not public; the 'frauds' such as will injure the limited community of traders, rather than society as a whole.

Towards the end of his book Defoe turns to consider 'the Dignity and Honour of Trade in England'. This topic involves a famous section illustrating the penetration of commercial families into the nobility and gentry, something even Wild or Peachum might have thought beyond his compass. He contrasts the effects of war with those of commerce, and rises to a characteristic Augustan high note:

> It is owing to trade, that new discoveries have been made in lands unknown, and new settlements and plantations made, new colonies placed, and new governments formed in the uninhabited islands, and the uncultivated continent of *America*; and those plantings and settlements have again enlarged and encreased the trade, and thereby the wealth and power of the nation by whom they were discovered and planted ... It is poverty fills armies, mans navies, and peoples Colonies ... The same trade that keeps our people at home, is the cause of the well living of the people here.
>
> (248-50)

Within five years George Lillo was to turn this into potent dramatic rhetoric: although some might detect in the reasoning of this passage some uncomfortable resemblances to Matt of the Mint's insolent remark, 'we retrench the superfluities of mankind' (II, i, 21). Defoe goes so far as to assert that the trader is a natural magistrate, who will be called on by others to settle disputes. He is 'the general peacemaker of the country'. This is in its way a noble concept of business: yet it seems oddly out of accord with the tone of the entire book—anxious, even desperate at times, unfailingly prudential. It is as though the civic dignity of a successful tradesman blinded Defoe to the actual mechanism of success.

Lamb archly enquired if Defoe might not have meant to satirise the morality of trade. There is no likelihood whatever that this was so. The ethic underlying this book became increasingly persuasive over the eighteenth and nineteenth centuries in Europe and America. And it needed a particularly shrewd writer, with a strong political animus to drive him, to reveal the shabbier implications of the code. Gay intuited that that 'application and industry' which Defoe sought to recommend could serve unworthy ends; and that 'knowledge and experience' were not confined to the honest. He had recent, if not living, proof in Jonathan Wild, executed in 1725 but three years later still the object of consuming public interest. The information laid against Wild had accused him of forming 'a kind of Corporation of Thieves, of which he was the Director' and of having 'divided the Town and Country into Districts, and appointed distinct Gangs for each, who regularly accounted with him for their Robberies'.[12] Defoe in his own life of Wild stresses this counting-house tidiness:

> He only kept his Compting House, or Office, like a Man of Business, and had his Books to enter every thing in with the utmost Exactness and Regularity.

Defoe further asserts that Wild might have 'carried on such a Commerce as this, with the greatest Ease, I do not say Honesty, in the World, if he had gone no farther ... So that in a Word *Jonathan's* Avarice hang'd him.[13] The concession 'I do not say Honesty' is significant. It betrays Defoe's awareness that the business ethic to which he subscribed might be said to underwrite qualities which (on his own showing) contributed to Wild's success. The moral, that Wild got carried away by greed and extended his depredations too far, is all of a part with the caution to the tradesman, not to reach out beyond his stock of capital too soon. (There is a section on rash 'Over-Trading'.) The biography of Wild appeared in June 1725, only three months before the first volume of *The Complete English Tradesman*. Perhaps Defoe worked too fast to see the possible relevance of Wild to his picture of the business world: probably he had already written most of the tradesman's manual when the career of Wild came to its spectacular end in May 1725.

But Gay was in a better place to see the links. When he drew up a portrait of the thief-taker under the name of Peachum, he invented a character oddly reminiscent of Defoe's paragon.[14] The world of *The Beggar's Opera* is one where even thieves 'act with conduct and discretion' (II, ii, 22). The greatest loser is Macheath, a supine *jeune premier* who has to be rescued from the gallows by a blatant dramatic coup—and it is he who believes that 'From a man of honour, his word is as good as his bond' (II, ix, 18). The modern realists—like Wild and Walpole—have a less chivalric concept of business. Their dramatic embodiment,

Peachum, is the true hero of this ironic fable. And he is what you get if you send the Complete English Tradesman into crime: or if the industrious apprentice goes into politics.

Notes

1. Jacob Viner, 'Satire and economics in the Augustan Age of satire', The *Augustan Milieu*, ed. H.K. Miller, E. Rothstein, G.S. Rousseau (Oxford, 1970), p. 93. Aspects of Gay's social satire are discussed in Peter Elfed Lewis, *John Gay: The Beggar's Opera* (London, 1976), pp. 41-58; and in various articles reprinted in *Twentieth Century Interpretations of the Beggar's Opera*, ed. Yvonne Noble (Englewood Cliffs, N.J., 1975). Standard guides are William Eben Schultz, *Gay's Beggar's Opera: Its Content, History and Influence* (New Haven, 1923; rptd New York, 1967), pp. 178-97; and William R. Irwin, *The Making of Jonathan Wild* (New York, 1941), esp. ch. i. The text and line-numbers used here follow those found in *The Poetical Works of John Gay*, ed. G.C. Faber (London, 1926; rptd New York, 1969). I have also consulted the edition by Edgar V. Roberts (Lincoln, Nebraska, and London, 1967), which contains helpful notes.
2. The bibliographical history of the work is exceedingly complicated. The first volume, directed to young tradesmen, appeared in 1725, with an expanded second edition the following year. A second volume was published in May 1727, eight months prior to the appearance of *The Beggar's Opera*. The text used here is that of the original volume, reprinted in Dublin by George Ewing (1726).
3. Cited from a letter of 1822 in *Defoe: the Critical Heritage*, ed. Pat Rogers (London and Boston, 1972), p. 86.
4. A 'rouleau' was 'a number of guineas, from twenty to fifty or more, wrapped up in paper, for the more ready circulation at a gaming table' (definition cited by Roberts, p. 64).
5. For example, Polly (I, x, 11); Robin of Bagshot, another cameo of Walpole (II, i 15); Mrs Coaxer (II, ix, 57).
6. George Theodore Wilkinson, *The Newgate Calendar* (London, 1962), I., 76-8. For further discussion of points raised in this paragraph see my book *The Augustan Vision* (London, 1974), pp. 101-3.
7. Cited from *Augusta Triumphans* by Schultz, p. 237.
8. See *Defoe: the Critical Heritage*, p. 86.
9. As well as synonyms like *bite, trick* and *fraud*, the word *cheat* itself occurs nine times in the play.
10. Quoted by Roberts, p. 14. See also the conversation of the women in II, iv; and note the mention of *contraband* and *duty* in Polly's song (I, viii, 99).
11. See Gerald Howson, *Thief-Taker General: The Rise and Fall of Jonathan Wild* (London, 1970), p. 168.
12. Quoted from the *Political State* by Irwin, p. 5. Bernard Mandeville similarly

argued that the profession of whoring should be rationalised, and brothels properly spaced about the town: see his *Modest Defence of Publick Stews* (London, 1724), esp. pp. 12-14. For a recent discussion with some relevance to the argument of this article, see M.M. Goldsmith, 'Mandeville and the spirit of Capitalism,' *Journal of British Studies*, 17 (1977), 63-81.

13. *A True and Genuine Account of the Life and Actions of Jonathan Wild* (1725), rptd in *Selected Poetry and Prose of Daniel Defoe*, ed. Michael F. Shugrue (New York, 1968), pp. 291-3. Wild's business efficiency became legendary—even Blackstone mentions it in his *Commentaries*, and it is treated in the Grub Street lives by 'Captain Charles Johnson', 'Captain Alexander Smith', and others.

14. See for instance Defoe's commendation of the 'methods' of commerce by which 'success' is achieved and the title of 'complete tradesman' earned (5). On the previous page Defoe emphasises the need for a trader to know where to dispose of his goods, another qualification Peachum abundantly possesses. For a recent view of the connection between business and crime in Defoe's mind, see Max Byrd, *London Transformed* (New Haven, 1978), pp. 17-24.

9

THE GUIDEBOOK AS EPIC
Reportage and Art in Defoe's *Tour*

It is thirty years since Godfrey Davies opened an article with the stark judgment, 'None of the larger works of Defoe has received so little actual attention as the *Tour*.'[1] This comment remains as accurate today. In the last three decades we have had the first collection of Defoe's letters, the standard bibliography, and one major biography—quite apart from a growing critical debate on the novels. This makes it all the harder to justify scholarly neglect of the *Tour*.[2]

Apart from anything else, *A Tour thro' the Whole Island of Great Britain* (1724-6) represents the author's mature literary artistry. Coming where it does in the canon, it draws on something more than his accumulated experience as reporter, spy, and social observer. It derives, too, from the creative enterprises which had occupied Defoe in the preceding five years. The truth is that the *Tour* functions in a more rewarding and inward fashion than has been generally recognised. Defoe gives us abundant documentation of English life, certainly. As we have seen in Chapter 4, there was a growing tourist market, and an appetite for guides. But the interest of the *Tour* is not confined to the social and economic data it provides. The book deploys the resources available to a great imaginative writer, and it supplies less a picture of Britain than a vision of nationhood.

The aim is to draw attention to three principal ways in which Defoe shapes his *Tour* so that it transcends mere guidebook status. One of these relates chiefly to structure, the other two concern the handling of language. Other aspects of the book's method would repay consideration; for instance, the question of point of view in the *Tour*, that is, the management of the authorial voice. Space forbids such enquiry here. As a final proviso, it should be noted that the argument of this chapter takes for granted one large assumption. The making of the *Tour* has never been thoroughly investigated, and its date of composition remains open to speculation. *A priori* it would be possible to hold that, since the book obviously includes material garnered twenty or more years earlier, it may have been substantially completed some time before publication. This is a matter to which I have given separate attention, and it is enough here to make explicit my broad conclusions.[3] These are that the *Tour* was indeed written from 1722 to 1725, and that Defoe's claim to have made a special journey for the purpose of his book was probably an honest one. If so, we are on firm ground in allocating the work to a period immediately after the composition of Defoe's celebrated 'imaginative' books—the novels, the *Journal of the Plague Year*, the *Memoirs of a Cavalier*— so long as we recall that the date of *their* composition is not very accurately known.

I

The first aspect of Defoe's literary skill manifested in the *Tour* relates to its structure. Now the immediate and, as it were, effective model for the book is supposed to be [John Macky's] *A Journey through England. In Familiar Letters* (1714-23).[4] One has only to glance at this work to see how defective is its organisation. Macky writes a series of short letters, many of which have no organic base as regards subject matter. A chapter finishes when Macky has used up enough pages, rather than when geographic necessity prescribes. London sprawls over from Letter IX in the first volume to Letter XIV, and turns up again in the second volume. Macky has to make a special 'excursion' to Bedfordshire: otherwise, as he remarks, it would have been left out. He digresses quite shamelessly on the state of the English language, improved by Sir Roger L'Estrange amongst others—the hack of Swift's *Tale* could do no more. Beleaguered in the Isle of Man, he calmly observes that he has omitted certain 'excrescences' and proceeds to fill the gaps. Cornwall might perhaps qualify for this description, stretching a point, but the Lincolnshire fens cannot be said to lie very far from the heart of the country. At this point, too, Macky introduces an account of the orders of society, more appropriate perhaps to the *Almanach de Gotha*.[5] Much more serious is the fact that Macky confines himself to largish towns and to the seats of the gentry. There is virtually nothing about the intervening countryside or about the route taken. In short, 'Journey' is a misnomer. What Macky gives us is a guidebook—a series of entries for places of interest. It would scarcely matter if the putative topographical framework were demolished, and the work presented as an alphabetical sequence—Blackheath, Blandford, Blenheim, Bodmin, Boston, and so on.

With Defoe everything is different. Not only does he maintain a clear itinerary, with the progress from one county to another carefully charted: he employs a number of shifts to give the reader a sense of movement. Prospects unfold as we pass through the country, landscapes emerge before our gaze and fall away, contrasting scenes follow one another in smooth succession. This is partly a matter of Defoe's greater visual acuity as compared with Macky's; but it has to do with fundamentals of his literary method.

From the outset of the first journey, it is evident that Defoe has a marked awareness of formal design:

> I began my Travels, where I Purpose to End them, *viz.* At the City of *London*, and therefore my Account of the City itself will come last, that is to say, at the latter End of my Southern Progress; and as in the Course of this Journey I shall have many Occasions to call it a Circuit, if not a Circle . . .[6]

Again, at the start of Letter V: 'As I am now near the Center of this Work, so I am to describe the Center of *England*, the City of *London*, and Parts adjacent' (I, 316). When Defoe added his third volume, partly in response to Macky's *Journey through Scotland* (1723), this second observation ceased to be literally true. But this does not affect the major issue: London is repeatedly described as the nexus of trade, society, fashion, wealth, and its fulcral position in the economic life of the nation stressed.[7] It is therefore appropriate that Defoe should construct his first two volumes round a series of trips to and from London, now in one direction, now another. The layout of the tour enacts the processes of human geography.

As the book develops, Defoe employs one crucial strategy to

forward this 'enactment' function. What he does is to choose expressions which apply both to the progress of his (in effect, fictional) tour and to the description which he is offering to the reader. Often this is simple enough—a matter of a single word ('But to return to my Passage up the River', I, 41).[8] It may be explicit in a passage of explanatory comment: 'I had still the County of *Cambridge* to visit, to compleat this Tour of the Eastern Part of *England*, and of that I come now to speak' (I, 77). On other occasions, there is a more complex and effective intermingling of the progress of the journey and the progress of the narrative:

> I now draw near to *Cambridge*, to which I fansy I look as if I was afraid to come, having made so many Circumlocutions beforehand; but I must yet make another Digression before I enter the Town; (for in my way, and as I came in from *New Market*, about the beginning of *September*;) I cannot omit, that I came necessarily through *Sturbridge Fair* ... (I, 80)

Here the term 'Digression' has much the force of a pun. It is through such linking devices that Defoe establishes the 'reality' of his tour, whilst at the same time advancing the course of his own narrative.

So vital is this bonding technique, and so important is simple repetition in Defoe's rhetoric, that further illustration is needed. At times, the author spells out the connection between his artistic plan and the actual route he is covering: 'From *Cambridge*, my Design obliging me, and the direct Road, in part concurring, I came back thro' the West part of the County of *Essex*' (I, 88). Sometimes Defoe appears to admit that the union of effects is a mere whimsical fancy, to be indulged but not believed: 'About four Miles, over those delicious *Downs*, brings us to *Epsome*, and if you will suppose me to come there in the Month of *July*, or thereabouts, you may think me to come in the middle of the Season' (I, 159). In places, the punning intent comes to the surface with conscious wordplay: 'My last Letter ended the Account of my Travels, where Nature ended her Account, when she meeted out the Island, and where she fix'd the utmost *Western Bounds of Britain*' (I, 254). The word 'digress' is exploited more than once, because of its ability to straddle journey and narrative: 'And, having mentioned *Andover*, though out of the

Road that I was in, I must digress to tell you, that the Town of
Andover lies ... (I, 289). A similar use is made of 'excursion', as at
the start of Letter VI: 'I have spent so much Time, and taken up
so much room in my Description of *London*, and the adjacent
Parts, that I must be the more cautious, *at least*, as to needless
Excursions in the Country near it' (I, 380).[9]

In this connection the motif of the 'tour' or 'circuit' mentioned
in the very first paragraph I quoted, is of special value to Defoe.
The word 'circuit' figures about thirty times throughout the
book. More than half of these occurrences are found near the
start or the end of a journey, where the narrator is most conscious
of his aims and means. A representative passage comes in Letter
VIII:

> The only Towns of any Note that are to be found on the North Bank
> of the *Trent*, are *Nottingham*, and the other *Burton*, of which I shall
> speak in their Order; at present, as I took a different Circuit in my
> Riding, I must do so in my Account of it also, or else if my Pen does
> not follow my Foot, I shall wander rather than travel, at least in my
> paper, whatever I did on my Horse. (II, 546)

A major part of the *Tour's* rhetorical energy is expended in the
ambition to make Defoe's pen follow his foot. Often this desire is
reflected in a direct appeal to the reader: 'I cannot but ... desire
you, my Friend, to travel with me through this houling
Wilderness in your Imagination, and you shall soon find all that
is wonderful about it' (II, 566). Even where apostrophe as such is
not in question, Defoe employs a sort of indirect address: 'It
would require a long Treatise of Commerce to enter that
[question]: But that I may not bring you into the Labyrinth, and
not show you the way out, I shall, in three short Heads, describe
...' (II, 613).

The most interesting development of the idea of the tour
occurs in Letter VIII also.

> Having thus passed the Rubicon (*Trent*) and set my Face
> Northward, I scarce knew which Way to set forward, in a Country
> too so full of Wonders, and on so great a Journey, and yet to leave
> nothing behind me to call on as I came back, at least not to lead me
> out of my Way in my Return. But then considering that I call this
> Work, a *Tour*, and the Parts of it, *Letters*; I think, that tho' I shall go a

great Length forward, and shall endeavour to take Things with me as I go; yet I may take a Review of some Parts as I came back, and so may be allowed to pick up any Fragments I may have left behind in my going out. (II, 552)

The most striking element in this paragraph is the constant interaction between what might be called topographic placing and narrative placing (note especially *passed, set my Face, set forward, leave behind, came back, out of my Way, in my Return, go a great Length forward, as I go, take a Review, going out*). It is apparent that Defoe effects the interplay chiefly through verbs and adverbial phrases. Throughout the work, indeed, he makes verbs do most to leap this aperture: 'But I must land, lest this Part of the Account seems to smell of the Tarr, and I should tire the Gentlemen with leading them out of their Knowledge' (I, 351). Or 'But though I am backward to dip into Antiquity, yet no *English* Man ... can go to *Carlisle*, and not step aside to see the Monument of King *Edward* I' (II, 687). Again, 'If I may straggle a little into Antiquity' (II, 508). A common adverbial formula is 'in my Course' (I, 299), which has the same capacity to look both ways.

By this means Defoe gives point and direction to his tour, so that it acquires a trajectory—something Macky's seriatim technique forbids. Even where he is forced into what could be an awkward explanation, he manages things far more adroitly and naturally than Macky, who seems clumsy and naive by contrast. A good example can be found in the second letter.

Here I remember'd that I had yet left the Inland Towns of the Two Counties of *Kent* and *Sussex*, and almost all the county of *Surrey* out of my Account; and that having as it were taken a Circuit round the Coast only, I had a great many Places worth Viewing to give an Account of; I therefore left *Windsor*, which was within my View, on one side of the River, and *Hampton Court* on the other, as being the Subject of another Letter; and resolv'd to finish my present View, in the Order I had begun it; *That is to say*, to give an Account of the whole Country as I come on; that I may make no incongruous Transitions from one remote Part of *England* to another, *at least as few as may be*. (I, 144)

This impression of taking the reader into his confidence comes to

Defoe's aid more than once. As for example, 'Before I go forward I should mention *Burrow Bridge*, which is but three Miles below *Rippon* . . . and which I must take in my Way, that I may not be obliged to go farther out of the Way, on the next Journey' (II, 627). Similarly in the Scottish portion: 'He that will view the Country of *Fife* must, as I said before, go round the Coast; and yet there are four or five Places of Note in the Middle of the Country which . . . must not be omitted; I'll take them as I go, though I did not travel to them in a direct Line' (II, 775). Once Defoe achieves an almost Shandean self-consciousness, when he comes to Chatsworth ('perhaps it shall be as many Years describing as it was in building, and the Description be no more finished than the Building' II, 582). Usually he stops well short of this, seeming content to dovetail the 'progress' of his journey and its literary analogue.

It would be possible to list a number of refinements on this basic technique. For example, various motifs are combined—in the third paragraph of Letter I, Defoe refers both to 'what I think, I may very honestly call a Circuit in the very Letter of it' and to 'some Little Excursions, which I made by themselves' (I, 5). Or he dramatises his double progression in a sudden vivid phrase: 'I am now at the Gates of *Edinburgh*; but . . . give me leave to take it in Perspective' (II, 707), or 'I am now at my Journey's End . . . I must now return *Sur mes pas*' (I, 242).[10] But these are sophisticated applications of a method that is in essence notably simple in proportion to its rhetorical utility.

Without disturbing the primacy of this particular constructional aid, Defoe introduced a number of other devices as the work progressed, again with the idea of promoting drive and impetus. In the second and third volumes especially, he made regular mention of the small 'compass' of his book as contrasted with the bulk of the material he had to cover. This served a number of rhetorical ends. It constituted a kind of apologia in the face of any observable defects or gaps in coverage. It stressed the plenitude of England, the sheer weight of phenomena to be encountered throughout the nation. This was a leading purpose of his tour, as I shall try to show in a moment. Third, the recurrent use of this notion—infinite riches in a little room—serves to reaffirm Defoe's ambition to create a literary vehicle appropriate to the material described. In this case, of

course, Defoe is saying it can't be done. The confines of the book
are too narrow to allow him to render the whole teeming
multiplicity of British life. But in deploring the particular failure,
Defoe is restating the general, or ideal, aim of his work. The
literary survey will be as faithful a copy as can be achieved of the
face of England: its failings result (the implication goes) from a
lack of space and from that alone.[11]

Some examples will make the point clearer. The word
'compass' occurs some fifteen times; scarcely any of these appear
in the first third of the book. Not surprisingly, Defoe's sense of
being hemmed in grows steadily more apparent as the book
proceeds. The first significant use comes at the start of the fifth
letter, when the author comes to speak of London:

> This great Work is infinitely difficult in its Particulars, though not in
> itself; not that the City is so difficult to be described, but to do it in the
> narrow Compass of a Letter, which we see so fully takes up Two large
> Volumes in Folio, and which, yet, if I may venture to give an
> Opinion of it, is done but by Halves neither. (I, 316)

Again we have the transference from narrational issues ('narrow
Compass of a Letter') to those of topography. For, within a few
lines, Defoe is writing that '*London* might, indeed, be viewed in a
small Compass' and then of the Roman walls ('Fifty Miles in
Compass'). Sometimes he uses the word as a simple spatial
term—'That Part of the River of *Thames* which is properly the
Harbour ... begins at the turning of the River out of *Lime-House*
Reach, and extends to the *Custom-house-Keys*: In this Compass I
have had the Curiosity to count the Ships' (I, 350). More
commonly, Defoe aligns the word with a term such as
'description', referring to his own constructional procedures. For
example, speaking of the Pool of London. 'In what Manner can
any Writer go about it, to bring it into any reasonable Compass?
The Thing is a kind of Infinite, and the Parts to be separated from
one another in such a Description, are so many, that it is hard to
know where to begin' (I, 349).

However, it is only in the second half of the book that this
emphasis becomes really insistent. Defoe became so conscious of
the idea that he extended it to time when writing the preface to
his final volume:

If all these Additions are to be found in the small Interval between the publishing the second Volume and this of the third, and that in so narrow a Compass, what may not every subsequent Year produce? and what Encouragement is here for new and more accurate Surveys of the Country? which, whoever travels over it, will always furnish new Materials, and a Variety both profitable and delightful. (II, 536)

On another occasion, Defoe turns a deft compliment on Burley in the Hill (rather nobly, as it was the house of his antagonist, the Earl of Nottingham) by utilising this ploy (II, 503). A similar passage occurs in the description of Alloway House, near Stirling (II, 800).

That last reference serves as a reminder that the Scottish sections are particularly rich under the aspect I have been considering. This may arise partly from Defoe's awareness that he was skimming over very large tracts of ground in a short space. Even though contemporaries were ignorant of the Highlands, and even though there was relatively little to detain the curious traveller (Wade's roads were only half-built anyway), there is a definite sense in the last part of the *Tour* that Defoe is anxious to get things completed. He may even have been under some pressure from the bookseller Strahan to cut down on space. Witness a remark in the introduction to the Scottish section:

Scotland is here describ'd with Brevity, but with Justice; and the present State of Things there, plac'd in as clear a Light as the Sheets, I am confin'd to, will admit; if this pleases, more particulars may be adventured on hereafter ... (II, 690)

A number of other hints can be found to support this line of argument, as for example the following:

From hence there is nothing remarkable till we come to *Aberdeen*, a Place so eminent, that it commands some Stay upon it; yet I shall contract its Description as much as possible, the Compass of my Work being so great, and the Room I have for it so small. (II, 808)

It seems to follow that Defoe's consciousness of restriction was greatest for opposite reasons, in the dense metropolitan area and in the scattered lightly populated outback regions. Judging purely by acreage, Defoe is about two hundred times more generous in space allotted to London and Westminster than to Scotland. But of course this reflects not just his own intent, but also the demographic facts of the time (London accounting for something like an eighth of the British population, higher than a century later)[12] and the taste of the age, when readers were no more interested in hearing about the natural splendours of the Highlands than Defoe was in gratifying such an interest.

It is possible that Defoe did feel himself genuinely cramped towards the end, but it is certain that he was capable of making abundant rhetorical capital from the feeling.[13] Nor does this sense of compression impair the structural identity of the book—its cleanliness of outline and purposeful trajectory. Macky, as remarked, makes a series of ill-charted trips in any direction that takes his fancy. He supplies no route: one moment he is in Ipswich, the next in Bury St Edmunds, and in principle there is no reason why his magic carpet should not loft him a moment later to Glasgow. Defoe, on the other hand, plans his itinerary so as to bring in the maximum amount of information as he goes—he likes the phrase *en passant* (for example, I, 350)—and so as to give the reader a definite impression of covering all the ground. Where Macky floats high over the landscape, Defoe hedgehops.

Finally, Defoe's tour is much more intelligently conceived than Macky's journey. Initially Defoe keeps to the idea of a 'circuit,' with London as the start-and-finish line. Letters I and II are complete in themselves. Letter V is a perambulation of the capital. Other trips occupy two letters: thus, III and IV describe a 'progress' to Land's End, out and return—similarly VI and VII with Anglesey the hinge of the journey. When Defoe reached his final volume, he obviously could not retain this scheme—a tour of Northern Scotland could hardly have its base camp in London (a good fortnight's travelling distant even as late as Culloden). What he did was to effect something of a compromise, but a sensible compromise. Letters VIII–IX–X all describe a route taken northwards from the Midlands, starting from the farthest point reached in earlier journeys—either the Trent or the Mersey. Scotland is simply parcelled up into three convenient units: XI, the border to the Forth, including Edinburgh, XII, the border to the Clyde, with Glasgow; and XIII, the circuit of the rest of Scotland, going counter clockwise on the map. As a result of these shifts in the third volume, the *Tour* loses a little in the way of symmetry of design. Yet it retains a shapeliness in its organisation that is far beyond Celia Fiennes, Stukeley, or Cobbett—not to mention John Macky. The following spatial diagram, crude as it must be, gives some approximation of the structural layout, viewed chiefly from a London base.

out	I	return
out	II	return
out	III	
	IV	return
London	V	Westminster
out	VI	
	VII	return
Trent—	VIII	Tees
Trent—	IX	Border
Mersey—	X	Border
Border—	XI	Forth/Clyde valley (E)
Border	XII	Forth/Clyde valley (W)
(E) Forth/Clyde valley	XIII	Forth/Clyde valley (W)

This complex interlocking pattern is beautifully adapted to Defoe's aim of comprehensive, yet intelligible, coverage. He has ordered his material so that the formal contours of the book mirror geographic, social, and economic reality. Literary expression and human ecology are wedded in the *Tour*'s grand design.

II

The second principal resource found in the *Tour* is broadly stylistic in character. Before it is allotted more detailed consideration, a few words on the style of the *Tour* as a whole will afford a useful background.

Defoe makes sparing use of the 'points' favoured by the more orotund eighteenth-century writers.[14] Antithesis, for example, that invariable standby of the less accomplished Augustan compiler, occurs rarely. The cases that are found are brief and effective, with no lingering or cleverness for its own sake: 'I that had read *Cotton's* Wonders of the *Peak*, in which I always wondered more at the Poetry than at the *Peak*; and in which there was much good Humour, tho' but little good Verse' (II, 564). A page or two later, at the Giant's Tomb, 'Here we miss'd the imaginary Wonder, and found a real one' (II, 568). In the introduction to the Scottish sections, we read, 'As I shall not make a Paradise of *Scotland*, so I assure you I shall not make a Wilderness of it' (II, 691).

Leaving aside oxymoron, to which I shall return later, there is only scattered and halfhearted use of parallelism; the best example occurring in the last journey:

> The Truth is, Cardinal *Beaton* was another *Sharp*, and *A*[rch]. *B*[ishop]. *Sharp* was a second *Beaton*, Alike Persecutors for Religion, Alike merciless in their Prosperity, and Alike miserable in their Fall, for they were both murther'd, or kill'd by Assassination. (II, 795)

More prominent is the use of epigram, although even here Defoe seldom places special emphasis on his own *bons mots*. His curt assessment of Bath theatricals provides a representative case: 'In the Afternoon there is generally a Play, tho' the Decorations are mean, and the Performances accordingly; but it answers, for the Company here (not the Actors) make the Play, to say no more' (II, 433). In a rather similar spirit: 'But Company and Diversion is in short the main business of the Place; and those People who have nothing to do, seem to be the only People who have any thing to do at *Tunbridge*' (I, 126). Of course, the very rarity of such a roundly phrased apothegm lends addd force when it does appear. Defoe from time to time gets ironic point from a well-placed parenthesis: 'It was a thick Mist, as is often upon those Hills, (indeed seldom otherwise) . . .' (II, 732). But this too is fairly uncommon.

Defoe habitually abjures finicky refinements of style, seeking a plain and direct way of writing.[15] His use of figurative language is in consonance with that aim. The *Tour* makes remarkably effective use of dead metaphor—stock images which pass almost unnoticed in reading but focus meaning sharply and neatly. Thus, Tilbury Fort 'may justly be looked upon, as the Key of the River of *Thames*, and consequently the Key of the City of *London*'

(I, 9)—the following paragraph amplifies this description, but without referring back to the particular figure of speech used at the outset. Again, Defoe speaks of the King's army marching over Scotland, 'not as a Foreigner and Conqueror, but as a Sovereign, a lawful Governor and Father of the Country, to deliver from, not entangle her in the Chains of Tyranny and Usurpation' (II, 805). He is not inclined to argue with the Jacobites; rather he lets the imagery carry its own disvaluing charge. The text is scattered through with such conventional locutions, adroitly employed to convey the precise weight and drift of emotion which Defoe wants.[16] We read of fear giving wings to news, of compliments with a sting in the tail, of throwing a veil over disagreeable facts, of fatal turns, of ladies shipwrecking their characters, of the Phoenix (of London) reviving, of money flowing and people settling like bees around a hive. The drugget trade makes an invasion on the broadcloth industry; facts are mastered, tempers bridled, darkness prevails in the remote Highlands, and the 'hot' rebels are always likely to spring. One chieftain was drawn into the snare of the late insurrection; others lacked stomach for the fight. In such ways Defoe quietly directs his readers' response to the facts he is presenting.

One highly personal aspect of the style is a tendency towards self-conscious mannerisms when a bold figure of speech is introduced. A point of land at Harwich 'as it were, laps over the Mouth of [the] Haven' (I, 34); the Isle of Ely 'look'd as if wrapp'd up in Blankets' (I, 80); whilst the wool trade in Wiltshire 'was first seated in this County, or, as we may say, planted itself here first, because of the infinite Numbers of Sheep' (I, 282). Sometimes we get a formula such as 'This, to use a Scripture Elegance, *is that City of Oxford*' (I, 396). In the region of Newcastle there are 'prodigious Heaps, I might say Mountains, of Coals' (II, 659). The caution with which the trope is brought into the account gives it an air of prudence and reliability—the reverse of that 'fabulous' quality Defoe so much distrusts.[17]

Orthodox simile is used in a similarly canny fashion. Commonest is the 'as if' formula: Orford was once a good town, but 'the Sea daily throws up more Land to it, and falls off itself from it, as if it was resolved to disown the Place, and that it should be a Sea Port no longer' (I, 54). At Epsom the horses race, 'flying over the Course, as if they either touch'd not, or felt the Ground they run upon' (I, 159). In Strathnairn, Defoe finds the lake contracted to the size of an ordinary river, 'as if design'd by Nature to give Passage to the Inhabitants to converse with the Northern Part; and then, as if that Part had been sufficiently perform'd, it open'd again to its former Breadth' (II, 817). For the rest, a favourite simile is that which compares a dockyard or industrial complex to a town or 'well ordered City'.[18] More ambitious is the picture of the remains and 'Trophies' of British antiquity, which 'are but, as we may say, like Wounds hastily healed up, the *Calous* spread over them being remov'd, they appear presently' (II, 663). The rumour of wild pillaging by the Irish dragoons in 1688 'spread like the Undulations of the Water in a Pond, when a flat Stone is cast upon the Surface' (I, 299). On Cannons, when Defoe may not have expected to be believed—or may not have cared if he was—he lets himself go: 'The whole is a Beauty, and as the Firmament is a Glorious Mantle filled with, or as it were made up of a Concurrence of lesser Glories the Stars; so every part of this Building adds to the Beauty of the whole' (I, 386). But such elegantly contrived nonsense is unusual in the *Tour*.

The metaphoric life of the book might surprise those who have combed the novels in vain for a sustained play of imagery.[19] The concrete force Defoe regularly attains can be gauged from a sample list of passages—Camden and Bishop Gibson have 'ransacked' the country for antiquities, yet Defoe can still glean 'Large Handfuls' they have missed. Colchester still mourns in the ruins of the civil war; the inhabitants of Harwich seem warm in their nests; Lord Castlemain was wounded by an arrow shot in the dark, that is, the South Sea Bubble. A cloud of canvas appears in the south coast harbours; merchants come to Epsom to unbend the bow of the mind; in the Welsh mountains Defoe converses with the upper regions; whilst at Chatsworth the mountains insult the clouds, intercept the sun and threaten the town. Money is melted into ale; trade is in a kind of hurry; and towns outswell their bounds.[20]

Two particular kinds of image stand out. The first might be described as anthropomorphic metaphor. Most common here is the use of the word *face* to mean aspect, appearance, show—'the face of wealth' and like expressions. This occurs over twenty times in the book, but a single instance may stand for all. The church at Sherborne 'is still a Reverend Pile, and shews the Face of great Antiquity' (I, 218). (Actually Defoe uses this word so freely he may have thought of it as a dead metaphor, as discussed above.) Closely analogous to this metaphor is the use of dress, often envisaged as bedizening an antique belle—Hampton Court 'put on new Cloaths, and being dress'd gay and glorious, made the Figure we now see it in' (I, 179). Exeter Cathedral is 'an antient Beauty' (I, 223); Defoe intends to refrain from 'loading [the] Work with Fragments of Antiquity, and dressing up the Wilds of the Borders as a Paradise, which are indeed but a Wilderness' (I, 253). Another striking image of this sort is the description of Leeds as 'what I may call the eldest Son of the Cloathing Trade in this County' (II, 606). This technique can easily be distinguished from that of ordinary personification. That figure occurs very rarely and then inconspicuously—at Market Harborough curiosity turns Defoe west, in Fifeshire Posterity will enjoy the sweets of the new interest in planting conifers.

A second group of images is made up of those connected with trade or commerce. In the light of Defoe's background, this is not very surprising, but it does seem more marked than in the fiction he was writing at this period. Phrases like the *gross* of the people, the *properties* (that is, qualities or attributes) of the gossiping part of the nation, speaking *in bulk*, *casting up*, and *computing*, abound throughout the work. Defoe's word for deceptions practised by an author is a *fraud*; he claims the *balance* (of accuracy) in his own favour; he says that a story is too old to have any *vouchers*, and that antiquity *claims the fee simple*. Sand *beggars* the soil, and (one of many legal turns of speech) facts come within the *verge* of the writer's knowledge. Epsom in the afternoon is like a trading town on holiday (though of course, as Defoe makes clear, it is anything but a hive of business activity); and Yorkshire grooms handle a curry-comb as deftly as a young scrivener does pen and ink. Particularly common is the use of *store* or *fund* in a figurative application; *stock* and *magazine* are also found, along with *treasure*, as noun and verb.[21] The word *business* itself is frequent, generally in the context, ''tis not the Business of this Work to enquire' (I, 158), along with similar locutions.

Everything up to this point would prompt the conclusion that Defoe uses language in a conservative and undemonstrative way—uses it well and pithily, no doubt, but without any obvious 'creative' ingredient in his idiom. There is, however, one rhetorical device which is ubiquitous in the *Tour*, and which goes a long way to give the book its character and its imaginative colouring. This is hyperbole.

It is ironic that the *Tour* has been left aside as prosaic and literal, compared with Defoe's fictional output. The truth is that, if anything, it is Defoe the novelist who sticks within the possible, and rates verisimilitude above what might be summed up by 'the marvellous'. The *Tour* is a sustained exercise in the marvellous. Sceptical as Defoe may be with regard to folk tales, he is warmly hospitable to 'wonders' of another kind. He is fascinated by extremes of scale, of volume, of age, of frequency, of wealth, of abundance, in short any distributable or variable feature of life. His rhetorical forms are driven constantly towards exaggeration.[22] Not, that is, the exaggeration of 'stretching' (as schoolroom slang puts it), where all figures are doubled and all exceptions quietly forgotten. Rather, Defoe exaggerates by seeking out and citing the extreme case. He does not necessarily falsify matters: he simply fixes his attention on the most striking data he can find. His *Tour* of Britain incorporates the function of a publication such as the *Guinness Book of Records*; he collects all-time highs like an avid cricket or baseball statistician. Arguably this is the common coin of journalism, but few pass the currency with such spendthrift profusion.

There are three ways in which this concern affects the words on the page: three varieties of hyperbole which sustain this rhetoric.

(A) The first is the direct superlative. Almost every paragraph in the three volumes contains a real or implicit superlative; I will take a single example, chosen pretty well at random (other passages would certainly show a higher density of cases):

> The best Ornament of the City [Chester] is, that the Streets are very broad and fair, and run through the whole City in strait Lines, crossing in the Middle of the City, as at *Chichester*. The Walls, as I have said, are in very good repair, and it is a very pleasant Walk around the City, upon the Walls, and within the Battlements, from whence you may see the Country round; and particularly on the side of the *Roodee*, which I mentioned before, which is a fine large low Green on the Bank of the *Dee*. In the Winter this Green is often under

Water by the Inundations of the River, and a little before I came there, they had such a terrible Land Flood, which flow'd 8 Foot higher than usual so that it not only overflowed the said Green, call'd the *Roodee*, but destroy'd a fine new Wharf and Landing-Place for Goods, a little below the Town, bore down all the Warehouses, and other Buildings, which the Merchants had erected for securing their Goods, and carried all away Goods and Buildings together, to the irreparable Loss of the Persons concern'd: Also beyond the *Roodee*, one sees from the Walls of *Chester* the County of *Flint*, and the Mountains of *Wales, a Prospect best indeed, at a Distance.* (II, 469)

In this paragraph of 219 words, Defoe employs (i) grammatical superlatives, as *the best Ornament, a Prospect best indeed*; (ii) grammatical comparatives, as *8 Foot higher than usual*; (iii) what might be termed implicit superlatives, as *very broad and fair, very good Repair, very pleasant Walk*; (iv) words connoting totality or absolute state, as *the whole City, the Country round, all the Warehouses, carried all away*; (v) terms of 'ultimate' state—this constitutes hyperbole (B), and is exemplified by *irreparable*; (vi) words whose semantic basis includes a superlative or comparative notion, as *fine large low Green, often under Water, such a terrible Land Flood*; and (vii) other phrases with an additive effect, as *not only . . . but . . . also.*

Some of these categories call for no special comment. As regards the method of the entire book, it should be noted that a common locution, *the most————*, may qualify for either (i) or (iii).[23] The most important class, however, in its bearings on the *Tour* at large, is item (vi). This is like (ii), except that there is no modifier such as *most, very, exceeding(ly)*. All the superlative force comes from within the lexical unit itself. Good examples are *prodigious*, which occurs over seventy times in the text along with *prodigy*, a rarer variant. The word commonly comes up in juxtaposition to nouns such as *sum, number, trade, increase, expence, quantity*. Each of these is a significant term in the idiom of the *Tour*, and several will be mentioned again. Another instance is the word *immense*, with its adverbial form. This comes about twenty times, generally with application to a noun like *estate, wealth, sum*, or the adjective *rich*. A third case is furnished by *infinite(ly)*. Here there are forty occurrences, often in relation to *populous, full, number*. Finally there is *exceeding(ly)/excess(ive)*; I have noted thirty usages, with *populous, rich, fine* common adjuncts. A number of other expressions turn up with slightly less regularity, but they serve a similar purpose. Amongst these are *eminent(ly)*, *extraordinary* (with *more than ordinary*, etc.), *monstrous(ly)* and *extreme* with its derivatives, all of which appear eight or more times. 'Monsters for Magnitude' (I, 347) is a noun-based variant.

For the rest, the true superlatives include two curious forms, *beautifullest* (twice) and *frightfullest*. In category (iii) certain adverbial phrases are of common resort, for example, *without exception, beyond (without) comparison, to the last extremity, heightened to such a degree.*[24] *A pretty many* is one unusual expression.

(B) The second mode of hyperbole I refer to as terms of ultimate state. The simplest form this takes is the verbal shape IN(UN)————IBLE(ABLE). Frequent examples are *incredible, innumerable, impossible, inexhaustible, invaluable.* Others I have noted more sporadically are *insupportable, indelible, unaccountable, irresistible, unpassable, indefatigable, intollerable, inexpressible, inestimable, invulnerable, inaccessible, impregnable, indissolvable* (of the Union with Scotland), *irreparable.* There are closely allied forms like *unprecedented.* However, Defoe can achieve the same effect with a phrase, for example, *all the magnificence . . . imaginable, in the fewest words imaginable* (a pure superlative, looked at in another way), *never to be exhausted, not to be matched, hardly to be valued, not to be described.* This last belongs to a group of negative formulae which Defoe uses freely: *so beautiful no pen can describe* is another variant. There is a strange concentration of these negatives in Letter V. Perhaps London seemed so vast and marvellous to Defoe that ordinary superlatives were inadequate. At all events, four pages concerned with the City of London (I, 340-4) supply more than half the book's quota of these phrases; the basic pattern is along the lines 'No Accounts in the World are more exactly kept, no Place in the World has so much Business done, with so much Ease . . . nobody is either denied or delayed Payment . . . nothing can be shewn like it in the whole World . . . no Sum is so great, but the *Bank* has been able to raise . . . nor can a Breach be now made on any Terms . . . nothing can be more exact . . . we see nothing of this at *Paris*, at *Amsterdam*, at *Hamburgh. . .*' and so on. All these are ways of connoting the *unparalleled* wealth/power/importance of Britain, a leading strategy of the *Tour.*[25]

(C) A third form of hyperbole resides in the stress laid on sheer multiplicity. There is a whole repertory of words to suggest repletion. They include *numerous, innumerable* and *not to be numbered, multiplied, crowd, throng,* as well as an odd little group of words *concourse, conflux, confluence, flux,* used of people—generally the gentry or polite society. More important under this aspect are epithets such as *considerable*[26] and *populous,* on which I shall speak further, and the verb *increase,* also reserved for the last section of this chapter. However, the main work is done by *quantity,* which astonishingly enters the text no less than two hundred times. (In passing, *quality* appears fewer than half a dozen times.) The phrase *vast quantity* accounts for twenty-four of these; *prodigious quantity* for twenty; and *great quantity* for eighty-four. The sheer iterative power of the word, hammering away through the entire book, contributes a great deal to the sense of abundance which Defoe is seeking. More than that, its overall density is backed by a few areas of high concentration, where the term is sown through the prose with almost reckless abandon. Usually these areas of the text are concerned with trade under one aspect or another. Thus, the famous description of Stourbridge Fair has fourteen instances of *quantity* in little more than two pages (I, 82-4). An even higher density occurs in the description of Clackmannan: the county produces not merely 'the best' coal in Scotland, but also—a far heavier stress—the 'greatest Quantity' (II, 801). Other passages showing heavy concentration include that on the Wiltshire woollen trade (I, 283-5: thirteen instances); that on the fisheries off the west coast of Scotland (II, 829: six occurrences within three short paragraphs); and that on the Milton/Maidstone district of Kent (I, 113-4: eight uses of *quantity*). In all these sections of the book, other words discussed here are prominent—for example, *prodigious, numbers, inexhaustible, populous,* and so on.

Just now I myself had recourse to the word 'abundance'. *Abundant* and *abundance* figure largely in Defoe's own writing: there are almost eighty examples. This is to a great extent explained by his fondness for the construction *abundance of,* meaning 'many'. The phrase has no article and takes a plural verb as a rule, seemingly by attraction from the noun governed—as, 'there are abundance of poor'. Defoe places little emphasis on the word, but it does provide further support for the rhetoric of quantity which underlies so much of the *Tour*.[27]

It might be thought that this unremitting stress on amplitude makes for a lack of artistic interest, as well as a sameness of texture in the prose of the book. An adverse critic might see the prominence of 'quantity' as against the latency of 'quality' in terms of Defoe's Puritan, middle-class ethos. This tropism towards numbers, substances, *Dinglichkeit*, rather than qualitative judgments, in certainly characteristic of Defoe at large. But while it may be wrong to see the *Tour* as a huge collection of Biedermeier furniture, lovingly put together out of a sort of acquisitive patriotism, beyond question Defoe's style relies heavily on this hyperbole of scale.

III

There is left what I take to constitute the main rhetorical ploy. The device involved is the repeated use of contrast, sometimes couched in terms of paradox. Basically what Defoe does here is to set off an idiom of growth—'rising' towns or 'flourishing' country—against counter-images of exhaustion—'barren' land or 'broken' remains.

Of course this is not the picture given us by most commentators on the *Tour*, who see it as a celebration of the new England. G.D.H. Cole, for example, writes with enviable confidence, 'Defoe's *Tour* is to be read, then, to-day above all for the light which it throws on the economic and social condition of England half a century or so before the coming of the Industrial Revolution.'[28] Cole believed that Defoe was at his best in describing 'what seemed to him really living and important', that is, 'the great social transition he saw proceeding around him'.[29] More explicit still is this passage:

> The things he looked for on his journeys were by no means those which appealed to the ordinary tourist of his day or our own. For 'antiquities' he had something of scorn; he liked towns which excelled not in the 'tumbledown picturesque', but in good, clean, well-built modern houses; he liked a countryside full of corn and cattle, rather than views and romantic wildness; and, above all, his interest was always in the present rather than the past. Not that he was unable to appreciate a fine old building or a 'view' which

conformed to his sense of beauty. But these were not the things he was in search of, and he gave them but a passing mention. What really interested him was the state of the country in a social and economic sense. (I, v)

Now this is a splendid account of the 'official' meaning of the book.[30] The deeper implications of the *Tour* run in a different course, however. Defoe, true, has a marvellously acute sense of *process*. And this comes out not only in his joyous welcome to the new commercial ventures of his day. He does write of the emerging order in graphic and warmly appreciative language. But he repeatedly sets against his picture of health and plenty an idiom of devastation. His *Tour* is pervaded by a sense of the fragility of human contrivances, very close to Pope's in that most central Augustan document, the *Epistle to Burlington*. Take the account of Dunwich in Suffolk:

This Town is a Testimony of the decay of Publick Things, Things of the most durable Nature . . . The Ruins of *Carthage*, of the great City of *Jerusalem*, or of antient *Rome*, are not at all Wonderful to me; the Ruins of *Ninevah*, which are so entirely sunk, as that 'tis doubtful where the City stood; The Ruins of *Babylon*, or the Great *Persepolis*, and many Capital Cities, which Time and the Change of Monarchies have Overthrown; these, I say, are not at all Wonderful, because being the Capitals of great and flourishing Kingdoms, where those Kingdoms were Overthrown, the Capital Cities necessarily fell with them; But for a private Town, a Sea-Port, and a Town of Commerce, to Decay, as it were of itself (for we never read of *Dunwich* being plundered, or Ruin'd, by any Disaster, at least not of late Years); this I must confess, seems owing to nothing but the Fate of Things, by which we see that Towns, Kings, Countries, Families, and Persons, have all their Elevation, their Medium, their Declination, and even their Destruction in the Womb of Time, and the Course of Nature. It is true, this town is manifestly decayed by the invasion of the Waters, and as other Towns seem sufferers by the Sea, or the Tide withdrawing from their Ports, such as *Orford*, just now named; *Winchelsea in Kent*, and the like; so this Town is, as it were, eaten up by the Sea, as above; and the still encroaching Ocean seems to threaten it with a fatal Immersion in a few Years more. (I, 54)

This is not an isolated purple passage. Throughout the book we get the same sensitivity to the depredations of time, in the manner almost of an Elizabethan sonneteer. It is this which gives tension and energy to what might otherwise be a perfunctory survey of 'the improving temper of the present age'.[31]

If one looks closely at the passage quoted, it is evident that the leading terms—the words and images which carry the principal emotional charge—have very little to do with anything Cole described. These include *decay, Ruins* (three times), *Time and Change, Overthrown* (twice), *fell, Decay* again, *Plundered or Ruin'd* (note the capitals, very rare here for verbs), *Disaster, Fate, Declination, Destruction, Womb of Time and Course of Nature, decayed* yet again, *invasion, sufferers, eaten up, encroaching, threaten fatal Immersion.* This is the vocabulary of elegy, or of a medieval *ubi sunt* lament (the idea of the wheel of fortune is very close), and not the language of confident social prophecy.

Since this conclusion departs so widely from the accepted view of the literary substance of the *Tour*,[32] a more detailed and scrupulous analysis of this idiom is plainly required. I shall take, first, the language of growth; second, that of decay; and third, the passages of juxtaposed imagery which, I shall argue, lend to the *Tour* its most distinctive artistic effects.

The vocabulary of growth, then, corresponds to that celebratory element in the 'official' *Tour*, located by Cole and others. It makes heavy use of words such as *plenty* (often with *vast*), *health(y), bounty, growing, prolifick, rise/rising, improve(ment), luxuriant, nourish, thriving* and so on. An important class of words is that of *flourish(ing), fertile, fruitful.* The first of these occurs some thirty times: in about ten of those cases *flourish* comes in immediate proximity to another key term, *increase.* As for *fertile*, it is found fifteen times, mostly in the first three-quarters of the book—Scotland, understandably enough in Defoe's terms, rarely inspires the word. *Fruitful* is more common, with forty instances spread quite evenly through the *Tour.* This compares with the most common term of general approbation implying a smiling landscape or a prosperous town—*pleasant*, which turns up over ninety times. This count is in some ways misleading—*pleasant* sometimes figures in a rather negative context, as where it is used four times in a description of the disadvantages from which the site of Edinburgh appears to suffer.[33]

The most significant individual word, however, is *increase*, either as noun or verb. (Defoe more commonly spells it with an initial *e*, though the variant *i* creeps in steadily towards the close.) This appears at least 140 times in the text, an extraordinarily high figure compared with its frequency in ordinary discourse.[34] In no author-concordance that I have checked with does *increase* figure amongst the fifty commonest words listed. Even if one included particles such as *and, the, of*, Defoe must use *increase* among his twenty commonest. Moreover, as with *quantity*, this overall dominance goes with exceptional density in specific regions of the text. Sometimes Defoe repeats *increase* with almost reckless unconcern. It occurs five times in ten lines in the description of refugees employed in Canterbury (I, 118). Exactly the same ratio appears in the entry for Bristol (II, 435), where *prodigious, flourishing, magnitude, swell'd* are also in evidence. Four instances at a short interval, allied with *prodigious, quantity, populous, number*, are found here:

> If they were so populous at that time, how much must they be encreased since? and especially since the late Revolution, the Trade having been prodigiously encouraged and encreased by the great Demand for their *Kersies* for clothing the Armies abroad, insomuch that it is the Opinion of some that know the Town and its Bounds very well, that the Number of People in the Vicaridge of *Hallifax*, is encreased one fourth, at least, within the last forty Years, that is to say, since the late Revolution. Nor is it improbable at all, for besides the Number of Houses which are encreased, they have entered upon a new Manufacture which was never made in those Parts before, at least, not in any Quantities, I mean, the Manufactures of *Shalloons* ...
> (II, 605)

There is something very revelatory about Defoe's adjustment of sense in 'which was never made ... before, at least not in any Quantities, I mean'. Literal nouns such as *trade* and *manufacture* call for little gloss, frequent as they are. The point about *increase* is that it is used in a whole gradation of meanings, from the literal to the quasi-figurative. Sometimes it is both subject and predicate, applied to persons and things, indicative and conditional, active and passive all at once:

> The *Manchester* Trade we all know; and all that are concerned in it

know that it is, as all our other Manufactures are, very much
encreased within these thirty or forty Years especially beyond what it
was before; and as the Manufacture is encreased, the People must be
encreased of course. It is true, that the encrease of the Manufacture
may be by its extending it self farther in the Country, and so more
Hands may be employed in the County without any encrease in the
Town. But I answer, that though this is possible, yet as the Town and
Parish of *Manchester* is the Center of the Manufacture, the encrease of
that Manufacture would certainly encrease there first, and then the
People not being there sufficient, it might spread it self further. But
the encrease of Buildings at *Manchester* within these few Years, is a
Confirmation of the encrease of People ... (II, 670)

Some degree of repetition might be put down to journalistic haste
or clumsiness. But nine occurrences in so short a space lead one to
the conclusion that Defoe is doing something analogous to poetic
reshaping—scrutinising a word as he repeats it, as with 'wit' in
the *Essay on Criticism*. There is an even greater huddle in the
account of Dumfries (II, 725). Here Defoe argues that the growth
of trade and the growth of population are interdependent. His
main rhetorical bridging device is the bare word *increase*.

This brings us naturally to another leading idea, generally
covered by *populous*. The word is endemic in nineteenth-century
gazetteers of Britain and America, and Defoe makes less personal
capital out of it than he does with *increase* or *quantity*. None the
less, a term which is not exactly ubiquitous in everyday speech
crops up a scarcely credible 120 times. One sign that the
expression carries a lower resonance for Defoe, despite its
currency, is the fact that it never appears in high
concentration—rarely more than twice in a given paragraph. It
is habitually found in conjunction with *exceeding(ly)* or with a
number of syntactically parallel adjectives—*rich, large, well-built*
and the like. *Populous* might have been considered above, along
with *abundance*, but it generally occurs in a 'growth' context,
whereas *abundance* is a routine trick of speech with Defoe and can
turn up anywhere.

Directly opposed to this set of terms we find a whole thesaurus
of 'decay'. The more regular expressions include *destroy/destruc-
tion*, often in conjunction with *time; loss, perish, exhaust, devastation*;
as well as *decrepid, sterile, desert*. In the later sections particularly
sink becomes an important antonym of *rise*.[35] *Remains* is common,

whilst *ruin* and its derivatives can be found forty-odd times. But much the most important single term is *decay* itself, with just over a hundred instances. Many of these form part of an oxymoron, with *growth* the contrary idea. But the word claims attention for its own sake, especially in the Scottish portions. This passage on Ayr does employ the growth-decay paradox, but the sheer iteration of this latter component stands out just as conspicuously.

> *Air* ... was formerly a large City, had a good Harbour, and a great Trade: I must acknowledge to you, that tho' I believe it never was a City, yet it had certainly been a good Town, and much bigger than it is now: At present like an old Beauty, it shews the Ruins of a good Face; but is also apparently, not only decay'd and declin'd, but decaying and declining every Day, and from being the fifth Town in *Scotland*, as the Townsmen say, is now like a Place forsaken; the Reason of its Decay, is, the Decay of its Trade, so true is it, that Commerce is the Life of Nations, of Cities, of Towns, Harbours, and of the whole Prosperity of a Country; What the Reason of the Decay of Trade here was, or when it first began to decay, is hard to determine ... (II, 739)

An equally marked concentration is found in the passage on Dunfermline, where Defoe spells out the 'threefold' decay of the town. The word occurs six times, along with *demolish'd, ruins, fallen* (in and down), *monuments, sinking, moulder'd away, injury of time, irrecoverable*.

As already indicated, this notion of decay is frequently associated with a sense of the lapse of time. Among the phrases used are 'time, the great devourer of the works of men', 'defac'd by time', 'Time has made it look gross and rough', 'the very ruins almost eaten up by time', 'defaced with age', 'sunk into time', 'sunk into their own ruins, by the mere length of time', 'to crumble, and suffer by time', and 'the meer injury of time'. At the end of Letter IX, Defoe allows himself a more sustained meditation on the ruins of time, in a vein quite different from anything Cole's description would suggest:

> I cannot but say, that since I entred upon the View of these Northern Counties, I have many times repented that I so early resolved to decline the delightful View of Antiquity, here being so great and so

surprising a Variety, and every Day more and more discovered; and
abundance since the Tour which the learned Mr. *Cambden* made this
Way, nay, since his Learned Continuator; for as the Trophies, the
Buildings, the religious, as well as military Remains, as well of the
Britains, as of the *Romans, Saxons,* and *Normans*, are but, as we may say,
like Wounds hastily healed up, the *Calous* spread over them being
removed, they appear presently; and though the Earth, which
naturally eats into the strongest Stones, Metals, or whatever
Substance, simple or compound, is or can be by Art or Nature
prepared to endure it, has defaced the Surface, the Figures and
Inscriptions upon most of these things, yet they are beautiful, even in
their decay, and the venerable Face of Antiquity has something so
pleasing, so surprizing, so satisfactory in it, especially to those who
have with any Attention read the Histories of pass'd Ages, that I
know nothing renders Travelling more pleasant and more
agreeable. (II, 663)

A short portion from this piece of prose was quoted earlier: but
the whole passage deserves notice, since it brings together so
many of the recurrent topoi I have considered. Nor is the
succeeding paragraph any less revealing: here Defoe adopts a
curious self-dramatising mode, full of the vocabulary of Puritan
discipline.

But I have condemn'd myself (unhappily) to Silence upon this Head,
and therefore, resolving however to pay this Homage to the Dust of
gallant Men and glorious Nations, I say therefore, I must submit and
go on; and as I resolve once more to travel through all these Northern
Countries upon this very Errand, and to please, nay satiate myself
with a strict Search into every thing that is curious in Nature and
Antiquity. I mortify my self now with the more ease, in hopes of
letting the World see, some time or other, that I have not spent those
Hours in a vain and Barren Search, or come back without a sufficient
Reward to all the Labours of a diligent Enquirer, but of this by the
way.

With its slightly chastened air of anxious self-inquiry, the tone
here is closer to that of Defoe's novels, particularly *Robinson
Crusoe*, than anywhere else in the book. Significantly, the extra
imaginative potency enters the *Tour* in the shadow of the ruins of
time.[36]
Third and lastly, Defoe's strategic contrast between the two

elements I have just considered, growth and decay. At its simplest, the device consists of a violent oxymoron set up within these terms. Thus we find *full perfection of decay* and *very perfection of decay*, with similar phrases. (There is an equivalent paradox used to underline the emphasis on *quantity*: several times, Defoe speaks of *an innumerable number!*) However, the opposition is often more elaborate and more interesting. 'If contraries illustrate ...', Defoe once muses (II, 583); and his technique does indeed rely heavily on the interplay of favourite Augustan anti-nomies—Nature and Art figured in the last quotation, and they appear together on half a dozen further occasions.[37]

Nevertheless, it is the contrast between expansion and contraction which most occupies Defoe. On the one side there is *overplus, enlargement*, the world of *profitable* and *delightful* activity. Set squarely up against this is the world of *neglect*, of *shattered* buildings and *desert* countryside. One pole connotes life, health, fecundity; the other suggests *dying of age, sinking into rubbish* (a surprisingly common noun), *burying beneath time*.[38] Images of *plenty, bounty, wealth*, are directly confronted by *disaster, calamities, delapidation*. Filtered through one set of terms, Britain is *populous, growing, prolific*: through the other, it is seen as *stript, sterile, waste*. The nation's treasure is *inexhaustible*, her citadels *so undemolished still* (I, 170, a strange locution). Yet in the same breath Defoe will show us mines *quite exhausted* or towns *all demolished*.[39]

There are some sixty passages in which this contrast is drawn out most explicitly. In my view they are the key sections by which the imaginative contours of the *Tour* are defined. The general character of their contribution to Defoe's purposes can be gauged from a sample survey. Apart from the passage on Dunwich already quoted, there is the carefully etched 'View of the Difference between the present and the past Greatness of this mighty City, called *London*' (I, 332); and the detailed comparison of English and Scottish palaces:

> *Greenwich* and *Nonsuch* are demolished.
> *Richmond* quite out of Use, and not able to receive a Court.
> *Winchester*, never inhabited, or half finished.
> *Whitehall* burnt, and lying in Ruins ...
> *Westminster*, long since abandon'd ...
> Whereas the Kings of *Scotland* had in King *James* the VIth's

>   Time all in good Repair, and in Use, The several Royal
>   Palaces ... (II, 776)

Of course, added force is imparted to this contrast by the fact that
it runs in the opposite direction from the prevailing antithesis
between prosperous England and economically backward
Scotland.

Defoe returns obsessively to this way of polarising the data
available to him. The town of Bideford has *flourished*; its twin, the
town of Barnstaple rather *declined*, because of an involuntary
rivalry (I, 260). Again, 'if we calculate Things present, by Things
past, the Town of *Minehead* is risen out of the Decay of the Towns
of *Porlock* and *Watchet*' (I, 268). The town of Ancaster *swelled* up
into a city, but is now *sunk* again out of knowledge (II, 501). York
is none the less beautiful because its ancient fortifications are now
demolished, 'for the beauty of Peace is seen in the rubbish' (II,
636). Appleby was once a *flourishing* city, but is now a *scattering,
decayed* and *half-demolished town* (II, 681: many other similar
examples). Haddington shows the marks of *decayed beauty*: it is
easy to see it is not what it has been, but an 'old half ruin'd, yet
remaining Town' (II, 700). Nothing will save Ayr from death, if
trade does not revive; Ludlow shows in its decay, what it was in
its flourishing estate. Defoe often extracts a wry humour from this
contradiction: at Worcester, he says, 'I went to see the Town-
House, which afforded nothing worth taking notice of, unless it
be how much it wants to be mended with a new one' (II, 443).
Whilst at Doncaster.

>   This Town, Mr. *Cambden* says, was burnt entirely to the Ground,
>   *Anno* 759, and is hardly recovered yet; but I must say, it is so well
>   recovered, that I see no Ruins appear, and indeed, being almost a
>   thousand Years ago, I know not how there should; and besides, the
>   Town seems as if it wanted another Conflagration, for it looks old
>   again, and many of the Houses ready to fall. (II, 589)

Abbotsbury, Defoe observes with contempt, is a town 'anciently
famous for a great Monastery, and now eminent for nothing but
its Ruins' (I, 214).

Two personal elements can be detected in all this. In the first
place, Defoe was obviously keenly interested in the process of

restoration after a disaster. It does not seem rash to attribute this to his own experience of the Great Fire and the subsequent rebuilding of London. Possibly one might see the Restoration of the monarchy, that crucial event for seventeenth-century Englishmen, as going some way to explain Defoe's perpetual recourse to phrases like 'a general Ruin a little recover'd (I, 118), or, of York, ''tis risen again' out of decay (II, 636). Of course, Defoe does explicitly refer both to the rebuilding operations and to the King's return; but it may be that his attitudes were affected at a deeper level too.

In the second place, there is a notable tendency to harp on the calamitous effects of the South Sea Bubble. As one who had twice known bankruptcy, it is to be expected that Defoe would have this recent trauma in the national experience strongly imprinted on his mind. All the same, Defoe seems even more obsessed by the topic than one would have anticipated. He just cannot keep off it.[40] And it is not simply that he mentions the Bubble and its effects so regularly: his writing takes on a special plangency at such moments, and the familiar imagery of growth and decay is invested with a poetry rarely found in his 'creative' work. For example, after dilating on the glory of the houses on the outskirts of London ('they reflect Beauty, and Magnificence upon the whole Country, and give a kind of Character to the Island of *Great Britain* in general'), Defoe turns to the wealth of the city which makes possible building on such a scale: but there is another side.

> It also would take up a large Chapter in this Book, to but mention the overthrow, and Catastrophe of innumerable Wealthy City Families, who after they have thought their Houses establish'd, and have built their Magnificent Country Seats, as well as others, have sunk under the Misfortunes of Business, and the Disasters of Trade, after the World has thought them pass'd all possibility of Danger ... (I, 169)

An even more lyrical passage on the 'Misfortunes of Business, and the Disasters of Trade' occurs at the end of the first letter. Defoe describes with enthusiasm Wanstead House, the home of the mercantile Child family, and then goes on:

> I shall cover as much as possible the melancholy part of a Story,

which touches too sensibly, many, if not most of the Great and Flourishing Families in *England*: Pity and matter of Grief is it to think that Families, by Estate, able to appear in such a Glorious Posture as this, should ever be Vulnerable by so mean a Disaster as that of Stock-Jobbing: But the *General Infatuation of the Day* is a Plea for it; so that Men are not now blamed on that Account: *South-Sea* was a general Possession; and if my Lord *Castlemain* was Wounded by that Arrow shot in the Dark, 'twas a Misfortune: But 'tis so much a Happiness, that it was not a mortal Wound, as it was to some Men, who once seem'd as much out of the reach of it; and that Blow, be it what it will, is not remember'd for joy of the Escape ...

This cannot be said of some other Families in this County, whose fine Parks and new-built Palaces are fallen under Forfeitures and Alienations by the Misfortunes of the Times, and by the Ruin of their Masters Fortunes in that *South-Sea* Deluge. But I desire to throw a Veil over these Things, as they come in my way; 'tis enough that we write upon them as was written upon King *Harold*'s Tomb at *Waltham-Abbey*, INFAELIX and let all the rest sleep among Things that are the fittest to be forgotten. (I, 90)

This is much more than a diatribe against the villainy of stock-jobbing. It outlines a little tragic plot, where pity and grief unite in a studied lament on the mutability of things.

How conscious was Defoe of what, on this showing, he was providing through the rhetoric of his *Tour*? Reasonably so, in my view. His preface announces at the very start all the leading themes—*the most flourishing and opulent Country in the World, a flowing Variety of Materials*, as well as *Novelty* opposed to *Antiquity*. In the third paragraph *encrease* turns up three times; other metaphoric terms include *luxuriance, harvest, face of things, glean, fruitful*. And by the second page, it is evident that the growth-decay syndrome is present in the writer's mind:

The Fate of Things gives a new Face to Things, produces Changes in low Life, and innumerable Incidents; plants and supplants Families, raises and sinks Towns, removes Manufactures, and Trade; Great Towns decay, and small Towns rise; new Towns, new Palaces, new Seats are built every Day; great Rivers and good Harbours dry up, and grow useless; again, new Ports are open'd, Brooks are made Rivers, small Rivers, navigable Ports and Harbours are made where none were before and the like. Several Towns, which Antiquity speaks of as considerable, are now lost and swallow'd up by the Sea, as *Dunwich* in *Suffolk* for one; and others, which Antiquity knew nothing of, are now grown considerable: In a Word, New Matter offers to new observation, and they who write next, may perhaps find as much room for enlarging upon us, as we do upon those that have gone before. (I, 2)

It would be otiose to list all the favourite items from Defoe's vocabulary here. Enough to recognise the general effect, which is distinctively Augustan—antithetical, elevated, sententious, *eloquent* to its nerve ends. One can hardly doubt that, in setting these pointed lines at the head of his work, Defoe knew what he was doing. This is the idiom of one habituated to *placing* things; to comparing, contrasting, sorting, and arranging experience. It is a rhetoric of process, which disposes and aligns facts within a historical sequence.

IV

A great deal of Defoe's own experience went into the *Tour*. Yet it is far from a direct transcript. Although there is so much shrewd observation of contemporary Britain in its pages, the inner momentum of the book derives from an astonishingly clear sense of history. Defoe reordered his personal memories, interlarding his own tours (made over half a lifetime) with borrowing from published sources. What he gives us is not a tour, straight, but the experiential equivalent of a tour. He imbued the work, too, with a crotchety, sometimes literal-minded poetry of his own. For this task he needed all his literary art, acquired not just as a great reporter, but as a great imaginative creator, too. So Defoe achieved the true English epic. (Significantly, it is a non-martial epic, perhaps closer to Virgil than Homer.)[41] His chosen vehicle was not that of the vainglorious *Brutiad*'s and *Boadicea*'s which men of the age so often projected, but the homely guidebook form, within which he dramatised his sense of the British nation, in its fullness and all its contrasting moods.[42]

Notes

1. Godfrey Davies, '*Daniel Defoe's A Tour through the whole Island of Great Britain*', *MP*, XLVIII (1950–1), 21–36. Davies's article is concerned with the various editions of the *Tour* which appeared until 1778. On scholarly and other reaction to the *Tour*, see also the introduction to my annotated abridgment of the work (Harmondsworth, 1971).

2. The only full-length study is that of Helmut Singer, *Daniel Defoe, A Tour through England and Wales. Eine kulturgeschichtliche Studie* (Leipzig, 1938), which confines itself to the English and Welsh sections. Singer's dissertation deals only with social and economic aspects of the *Tour*: Part I, with *Die Gesellschaft*, Part II, with *Die Landwirtschaft*. It relies on obsolete sources and contributes virtually nothing to a literary understanding of the book.

3. In two articles I have set out in detail the reasons for this dating. See *Bulletin of the New York Public Library*, LXXVIII (1975), 431–50; and *Prose Studies*, III (1980), 109–37. There is abundant evidence that Defoe must, at the very least, have carried out a full-scale revision of the *Tour* as late as the year of publication—1724-25-26 respectively for the three volumes.

4. This is the title of the first two volumes (1714, 1722). The third volume appeared as *A Journey through Scotland* (1723).

5. See Macky, *Journal*, II, 223 ff., 231 ff., 236 ff.

6. Defoe *Tour*, I, 5. All quotations follow this edition, except that long *f* has been normalised to *s*. The Everyman text now includes the Scottish sections and an introduction to these by D.C. Browning; the separate introduction which Cole wrote for this edition has been retained. Reference to the Everyman volumes (London, 1962) is in the form T/B. Where a quotation covers two or more pages, only the first page is cited.

7. Cf Singer, p. 21.

8. For similar usages, cf. I, 249, II, 682. In an age of computerised literary study, it should be added that my word-counts are 'hand' calculations, which means they are likely to be underestimates.

9. Other occurrences of 'excursion' are at II, 467, 539, 765, 802.

10. Cf. II, 468, 'As I am now at *Chester*, 'tis proper to say something ...'

11. Compare the very first words of the book: 'If this Work is not both Pleasant and Profitable to the Reader, the Author most freely and openly declares the Fault must be in his Performance, and it cannot be any Deficiency in the Subject' (I, 1).

12. Depending on how one establishes the bounds of London, and whose figures one trusts, one can arrive at different population figures from three-quarters of a million upwards. In 1725 the total for greater London—that is, the City and Westminster with the outparishes, plus Southwark—may have been approaching the million mark. Defoe's estimate (I, 324) is 'at least, Fifteen Hundred Thousand'. This is certainly too high; but it is worth remembering that Defoe would organise his *Tour* according to this belief. See E.A. Wrigley, 'A simple model of London's importance in changing English society and economy 1650-1750', *Past and Present*, XXXVII (1967), 44–5, and H.J. Habakkuk, 'English Population in the

Eighteenth Century', *Economic History Review*, VI (1953), 117–33.

13. Other rhetorical formulae encountered are suggested by these quotations: '*Harwich* is a Town so well known, and so perfectly describ'd by many Writers, I need say little of it' (I, 34); 'I could say much more to this Point, if it were needful and in few Words could easily prove ...' (I, 44); 'I can't omit, however little it may seem ...' (I, 59); 'To all this I must add, without Compliment to the Town, or to the People, that the Merchants ... of *Yarmouth* have a very good Reputation in Trade' (I, 68); 'At the entrance of a little nameless River, scarce indeed worth a Name, stands *Whitby*' (II, 656).

14. Despite this, the *Tour* is of course written chastely and well for the most part. One of the oddest lapses comes early on, with a horrible burst of alliteration, mainly on sibilants, which Defoe can scarcely have read aloud to himself:

> 'Tis on this Shoar, and near this Creek, that the greatest Quantity of fresh Fish is caught, which supplies not this Country only, but *London* Markets also: On the Shoar beginning a little below *Candy Island*, or rather below *Leigh* Road, there lies a great Shoal or Sand called the Black *Tayl*, which runs out near three Leagues into the Sea due East; at the End of it, stands a Pole or Mast, set up by the *Trinity-House* Men of *London*, whose business is, to lay Buoys, and set up Sea Marks for the Direction of the Sailors; this is called *Shoo-Bacon*, from the Point of Land where this Sand begins, which is call'd *Shooberry-Ness*, and that from the Town of *Shooberry*, which stands by it. From this Sand, and on the Edge of *Shooberry*, before it or South-West of it, all along, to the Mouth of *Colchester* Water, the Shoar is full of Shoals and Sands, with some deep Channels between; all which are so full of Fish, that not only the *Barking* fishing-Smacks come higher to Fish, but the whole Shoar is full of small fisher-Boats in very great Numbers, belonging to the Villages and Towns on the Coast, who come in every Tide with what they take: and selling the smaller Fish in the Country, send the best and largest away upon Horses, which go Night and Day to *London* market (I, 11).

15. 'True Protestant Plainness' is Defoe's own phrase for the London churches (I, 334).

16. Apart from the instance quoted in the text, typical cases are use of 'Bowels' (of the earth), I, 265, II, 802, 827; the word 'bubble' for cheat or defraud (II, 786)—a commonplace expression at that time; and 'province' in such phrases as 'it is not my province' (I, 382, II, 617, 665).

17. Two examples among many of this sceptical attitude are found at I, 185, 188.

18. See I, 108, 138 (Portsmouth docks, as 'a kind of Marine Corporation', 193 (Wilton House as 'a well govern'd City', and the Earl of Pembroke as 'a true *Patriarchal Monarch*, reign[ing] here with an Authority agreeable to all his Subjects (Family)'—the explanatory parenthesis is characteristic of Defoe's suspicious handling of metaphor).

19. Closer to the cadence and accents of Defoe's fiction is this, from the start of Letter IV:

> There was another Difficulty also, upon which my Navigator, or
> Commander, as I called him, who was an old experienced Seaman,
> dissuaded me from the Undertaking; and that was the Necessity of
> getting Pilots to every Part of the Coast, and to every Port, River, and
> Creek, and the Danger of not getting them: The Necessity was plain;
> For that, as I proposed to keep all the Way near, or under the Shore, to
> enter into all the Bays, and Mouths of Rivers, and Creeks, as above: 1.
> It would be impracticable to find any single Man that knew so perfectly
> the whole Coast, as to venture without Pilots. 2. Pilots would not always
> be found, especially on the *North* and *West* Coasts of *Scotland*; so I laid it
> aside, I say, as a hopeless, and too dangerous Adventure, and satisfied
> myself, to make the Circuit very near as perfect by Land, which I have
> done with much more Pains and Expence; the Fruit of which, you
> have, in Part communicated in these Letters (I, 254).

Not just the content and vocabulary, but the general mode of utterance,
with its painstaking effort to weigh competing alternatives, strongly recalls
Captain Singleton. See for instance pp. 113-14 in the Everyman edition, ed. J
Sutherland (London, 1963).

20. I, 2, 7, 16, 36, 90, 123, 160; II, 458, 527, 583, 797.
21. Defoe also speaks of 'pay[ing] the Debt of a just and native Writer' (I, 2),
    and 'pleading' antiquity (II, 548). *Vast stock* occurs several times;
    inexhaustible store(-house) at least six times, quite apart from *treasure not to be
    exhausted* and the like. There could hardly be a more quintessential
    Augustan image.
22. Hyperbole of an orthodox cast—'almost every Gentleman's House is a
    Castle' (II, 682)—is quite common also. Cf. I, 384 (Hampstead Heath is 'so
    near Heaven' that only a race of 'Mountaineers' could live there!), as well
    as I, 391; II, 807. Cf. T.S. Ashton, *An Economic History of England: The
    Eighteenth Century* (London, 1955), p. 33: 'Defoe had an eye for whatever
    was striking or unusual, and sometimes, he ran to hyperbole . . .'.
23. *Utmost* appears in one way or another on at least ten occasions, generally in
    combination with a word like *extent*. A strange phrase employed is 'so every
    where' (I, 162).
24. Variants are *to an extreme, to perfection*. Another mode of emphatic
    superlative is attained simply by accumulation: 'the first, and best, if not
    the only Haven' (I, 256).
25. Cf. also II, 427:

> Nor can any Nation in *Europe* show the like Munificence to any
> General, no nor the greatest in the World; and not to go back to antient
> times, not the French Nation to the great *Luxemberg*, or the yet great
> *Turenne*: Nor the . . . yet greater Duke of *Lorrain* . . . I say none of these
> ever receiv'd so glorious a Mark of their Country's Favour

as did Marlborough in the shape of Blenheim.
26. This word appears over seventy times. Defoe possibly thought it was not an

impressive term without a modified; *very considerable* is the commonest usage.

27. *Abound* is employed in a few places, normally in proximity to 'growth' clusters involving *flourishing* and the like.

28. T/B, I, vii. For a similar judgment, compare *Tour*, I, ix: 'It is, then, primarily as a guide to social economic conditions that De Foe's *Tour* is important.'

29. T/B, I, vi, vii.

30. I use the epithet in the sense developed by Thomas R. Edwards, *This Dark Estate* (Berkeley, 1963), p. 6 and passim.

31. *Tour* (I, 44). Surprisingly, *improve(ment)* itself is not especially widespread in the text.

32. Cole enunciates the traditional view well enough:

> Here then I leave the *Tour*, making for it no extravagant claim as a work of exceptional genius, but rather suggesting that its very plainness and the humble purpose it was designed to serve give it a special value as a work of historical record. It is well written, in clear quickly-moving sentences that make it easy and pleasant reading. That is all De Foe tried to make it (*Tour* I, xxiv).

The same notion of Defoe's plain and artless style appears in Esther Moir's account: 'Defoe in contrast [to Celia Fiennes] writes a straightforward narrative prose, cold, critical and measured, scorning to indulge in the hyperboles with which her work is adorned' (*The Discovery of Britain* [London, 1964], p. 36). My own analysis prompts an opposite conclusion on all issues raised here, as regards Defoe; even the word 'critical' may need some qualification.

33. (II, 710). Other relevant items of 'growth' vocabulary are *glut, overgrown, throng, multiply*.

34. *Increase* does figure in *A Journal of the Plague Year*, but by no means so prominently. *Spread*, on the other hand, appears to be relatively more common in the *Journal* than in the *Tour*.

35. A representative context for *sink* is this: 'But now things infinitely modern ... are become Marks of Antiquity; for even the Castle of *York* ... is not only become antient and decayed, but even sunk into Time, and almost lost and forgotten: Fires, Sieges, Plunderings and Devastations, have often been the Fate of *York*; so that one should wonder there should be any thing of a City left' (II, 636).

36. Esther Moir writes, 'Defoe's determination not to be led astray from his avowed purpose of studying the present day into the delightful view of antiquity, has deprived us of what would undoubtedly have been refreshingly sane and balanced descriptions' (p. 45). This is to take Defoe's protestations too literally; his need to *resolve* and *mortify himself* arises from his inability to stick to his declared objectives. Actually the *Tour* never holds to this self-denying ordinance for longer than a page or two at a time.

37. A well-known instance occurs in the description of Bushey Heath: 'It was

all Nature, and yet look'd like Art' (I, 388). See also II, 581. *Nature* is sometimes used in a personified sense.

38. Defoe speaks of 'the Corps of the old *English* Grandeur laid in State' (I, 365), by which he means the 'ruin'd Antiquity' of the Palace of Westminster.

39. *Abate* and *decline* also figure on a number of occasions, e.g. II, 449. *Depredated* occurs at I, 187.

40. Cf. I, 37, 346. Defoe also makes a number of references to the ruin occasioned by the stop of the exchequer in 1672, e.g., I, 353.

41. Cf. my article, 'Defoe and Virgil', *English Miscellany*, XXII, 93–106.

42. For a different view of some of the issues raised in this chapter, see Geoffrey M. Sill, 'Defoe's *Tour*: Literary Art or Moral Imperative?' *ECS*, XI (1977), 79–83. The most important recent study is Alistair M. Duckworth, 'Whig Landscapes in Defoe's *Tour*', *PQ*, LXI (1982), 453–65. A full discussion of the matters explored by Duckworth's essay would extend this chapter beyond proper bounds.

10

'THIS CALAMITOUS YEAR':
A Journal of the Plague Year and the South Sea Bubble

I

In October 1720, as fears rose in England that the dreaded bubonic plague would spread from Marseilles, Daniel Defoe wrote an article for Applebee's *Weekly Journal*.[1] It was in the character of a Leicestershire grazier, who had come up to London a month before, and who had been impressed by the bustle and smartness of the city, particularly around Threadneedle Street. He proceeds with his story:

> I took my Walks again over those Places but yesterday, and tho' I found the Crowd was as great as ever, yet I found such a strange Alteration in the Folks, that I am frightened at them. It is true, upon *Change* among the Merchants, I could see little or no Alteration; but when I came *athwart the Street again*, I saw the strangest Alteration that ever I saw in my Life in the People; and I concluded they were not the . . . Men that I saw before, for they were a jolly, merry sort of People; but I concluded these were either some honest sorrowful Persons, come together to some great Burial, and so they had put on the most dismal Countenances they could frame for themselves; or, that some Sickness was broke out in the Place, and these walking Ghosts were all infected with the Plague; for never Men look'd so wretchedly.

The grazier encounters a man wringing his hands, and crying out, 'I am undone!' When he reaches Threadneedle Street, things are even worse. A desperate individual is pointed out to him, marked off by his fearsome appearance; 'he looks Pale, Frighted, Angry, and out of his Wits'. It is a vision of a city in the throes of some appalling visitation.[2]

Given the date and the subject-matter, one might be forgiven for relating the article to Defoe's known concern for public health. It would be easy to read the passages I have quoted as a

151

trial run for *A Journal of the Plague Year*, published less than eighteen months later. They could be seen as a first fictional attempt to rouse public awareness of the dangers of infection: a publicity campaign Defoe was to mount in the press and in his pamphlet, *Due Preparations for the Plague*, published a month earlier than the journal. One would see the lamentations, the hints of a 'great Burial' and the frightened individuals out on the street as characteristic features of a city in the throes of a convulsion such as the Plague of London in 1665.

All these plausible conjectures would be wholly wrong. In the long quotation I provided, one necessary tactical step was to insert an aposiopesis after the words 'I concluded they were not the ...' The full passage runs, 'they were not the *Bubblers*, and *Stock-jobbers*, and *South-Sea* Men that I saw before'. I neglected to mention that Threadneedle Street included South Sea House. In fact the article is not, ostensibly anyway, concerned with the threat of plague at all. It is a semi-comic treatment of quite a different subject: the aftermath of the South Sea Bubble, which had burst with shattering effect a few days earlier. One bemused investor had written during the previous week: 'There never was such distraction. You can't imagine the number of families undone ... many a £100,000 man not worth a groat, and it grieves me to think of some of them.'[3] The story in Applebee's *Journal* indeed portrays a moment of national crisis—but the crisis was financial, not sanitary, in nature.

In the same issue of the newspaper another item consisted of reports on the breakdown of communal life in Marseilles as the plague took a stronger hold. It is reprinted by William Lee as the work of Defoe, along with the grazier's narrative, and the attribution is entirely plausible. Throughout 1720, 1721 and 1722 two stories dominated the columns of the London press: the plague and the Bubble. Each threaded in repeatedly with the other, and there is strong evidence that Defoe's day-to-day journalism involved him in regular coverage of both the continuing sagas. The climax was reached first in respect of economic matters, when the Bubble burst in the autumn of 1720. The outbreak of plague in Provence, already well established, lingered on into the following year. But in both cases, the aftermath was as important as the event itself. Defoe spent almost two years propagandising in favour of government plans to curb the onset of the plague;[4] similarly he supported the efforts of the ministry under Robert Walpole to reconstruct the national economy. (He could reasonably claim to be one of those who had foretold the imminence of a crash after the unguarded expansion of the credit machine in recent years.)[5] The two stories thus continued to run in parallel, and both remained at the centre of public awareness when the *Journal* was published in March 1722.

In the best edition of the *Journal* we possess, Louis Landa has noted how 'in the pages of several periodicals, *The Daily Post*, *Applebee's Journal*, and *Mist's Journal*. [Defoe] took occasion no fewer than ten times within the year to describe the horrors and ravages of the plague in France'. He adds the significant comment: 'No other historical event so captivated the mind and imagination as did the awesome Plague of London.'[6] These statements are true; but they will bear a rider. First, it should be noted that Defoe was writing for exactly the same papers at exactly the same time a series of items on the Bubble and its aftermath. Second, the only historical event that rivals the Plague in resonance during the last period of Defoe's career is the Bubble. At least ten separate published books which he produced in the 1720s make some reference to the episode; and several, as we have just seen with reference to the *Tour of Great Britain* and the *Complete English Tradesman*, have a constant undertow of allusion.

We can stay with Landa's account of the *Journal* and see how the double application continues to operate:

> Not least in significance is that the tragedy of 1665 was a tragedy of London, a city of perennial fascination to Defoe. There was something voracious in his relation to the metropolis, a zest for every aspect of it, inns, streets, markets, buildings, its beauty *and* its ugliness, that often generates a lyrical energy in his prose when London is the subject ... What appealed to him most of all was the spectacle of a teaming, bustling, dynamic city, infinitely complex, a pageant of movement and colour, splendid despite its tawdry aspects, impressive and intricate by virtue of the intertwining of the lives and fates of its massive population. What the Great Plague of 1665 presented to Defoe's imagination was London in a wholly different guise, diametrical and yet fascinating in the very magnitude of the change, its vitality withered.

And again, a little further on:

> The real tragedy is corporate. It applies less to this or that person or family, more to the greater organism, the stricken city ravished by plague, its people either fled or dying, its marts closed, its vast energies replaced by silence or inaction.

Landa sees the *Journal* as 'a historical narrative of London in a year of agony', and goes on to relate its form to the literary genre dealing with floods, earthquakes and comets.[7] He sees, that is, the plague as a natural calamity which could be viewed in terms of convulsions in the entire frame of the macrocosm—much as Defoe's earlier collection *The Storm* had viewed the tempest which hit England in 1703.

But again it bears insistence that the phrase 'a year of agony' fits with absolute precision the events of 1720 in the economic and political sphere. The financial drama was likewise played out in London, for though investors and annuitants might be spread around the country, the key actors were all in London and the crucial moments were witnessed in the capital. One of the effects of the financial revolution that helped to foster the Bubble was to centralise power in London: the creation of the Bank of England, the development of the great trading institutions like the united East India Company and the South Sea Company itself, the growth of sophisticated machinery for insurance, credit and investment—all these made the City of London into a money market of European importance. In earlier centuries Venice or Amsterdam had stood far ahead in this realm of human activity; now the great modern metropolis, like Paris and London, had outstripped the specialised centres. The Bubble was a tragedy of corporate London, above all of the City of London.

A further objection that might be raised is that the Great Plague dealt in death, the Bubble in nothing more than financial undoing. To this there are three answers. The first is that the economic collapse did bring in its wake a spate of suicides. It even became possible to insure against killing oneself. There are frequent reports in the press of such events: for example, on 29 October 1720 *Applebee* told of a woman 'of Distinction' who had hanged herself, 'the Cause whereof is said to be the great Fall of South-Sea Stock'. A frustrated hanging had been described, just a week earlier. Another case was reported in the same paper on 7 January 1721, and again the paper adds, 'This unfortunate Accident was occasion'd by the Fall of the South Sea.' Examples could be multiplied,[8] and this without appealing to the best-known cases in which principals in the affair were reduced to suicide. James Craggs senior, who took laudunum in March 1721, is the most striking example. That Defoe was fully aware of such acts can be confirmed from the *Tour*, where he mentions a number of cases, some perhaps from first-hand knowledge.[9]

The second answer to the objection is that the South Sea disaster brought with it a widespread decline and a 'freeze' in activity. Individuals were wiped out, not just in terms of wealth, but also in terms of social standing. Defoe had admired the vigour of mercantile London, and this was destroyed when the Bubble burst. The contrast between a former bustling confidence and a miserable torpor applied in 1720, just as in 1665; it is explicitly drawn by the Leicestershire grazier in the issue of Applebee's paper from which we started.

The third rejoinder is the most interesting from a literary standpoint. It soon became evident that the vocabulary of sickness was widely felt to be the most appropriate for the effects of the Bubble. Words such as disease, distraction, distemper, medicine, recovery, and so on, are in regular employ. Sometimes from the imagery used it is hard to know whether a newspaper story concerns the plague, the financial collapse, or both:

Exchange-Alley sounds no longer of Thousands got in an Instant, but on the contrary, all corners of the Town are filled with the Groan's of the Afflicted (*Mist*, 1 October 1720).

We hear that some other tottering Tradesmen arre preparing to take this Opportunity to go off with a Bon Grace (*Applebee*, 15 October 1720).

To imprison an undone Gentleman, or a ruin'd Tradesman *NOW*; or to keep them confin'd that are already shut up, is it not like murdering those that are Sick of the Plague? The Distemper has been a Visitation; *South-Sea* has been a Judgment from Heaven; Shall we not pity them whom God has smitten? . . . When shall the Cries of the Prisoners be heard? (*Applebee*, 15 April 1721).

The last example is noteworthy, in addition, for its demonstration that the Bubble could be assimilated to the same pattern of providential intervention as the stories of natural calamity mentioned by Landa. Its use of confinement imagery also looks forward to the *Journal*.

How conventional this equivalence became we can see from a number of extended examples of the trope. In *Applebee* for 17 December 1720, the writer argues that 'if this Blow to Publick Credit is carry'd on much farther, I fear it may indeed be fatal to the whole Kingdom'. His case proceeds:

> In a sick Body, when the Mass of Blood is corrupted, when the Constitution of the Body is subverted, and the Motion of the Spirit stop'd and stagnated, the Patient finds no Benefit by Medicine; he must be left to the Secret Operations of Nature, either for Life or Death. The Body of the South Sea People seem to be in just such a Crisis at this Time; the Distemper is strong upon them,—they sink under it, and 'tis vain to offer Reasons or Arguments to them; the Patient must be left to Nature, and to the ordinary Operation of his own demented Understanding.

The writer goes on to pursue 'remedies' for this situation, and congratulates parliament on its efforts to 'relieve' and 'recover' the nation. It was convenient political rhetoric to describe the Bubble as a shock to the system, from which only wise government would rescue the patient. (Compare the prudent action of the authorities in the *Journal*.)

It is virtually certain that Defoe wrote this last item, and almost equally so in other cases. Day by day he would be penning paragraphs to this sort of effect: 'Paris, October 28. Our Disasters, occasion'd by the Reduction of Bank Bills, encrease every Day, and are esteem'd a Calamity second to, tho' not equal, with the Plague.' The recognition that 'the *South Sea* Affair is now become a general Calamity' was commonplace, and it provoked much journalism along these lines, concerned with the state of insolvent debtors:

> Did ever any Nation refuse People infected with the Plague, the Liberty of a Pest House, or Lazaretto? Did the Magistrates of *London* complain of breaking down the Walls of *Moorfields*, and of People's Trespass in carrying their Goods thither, to save them from the

Flames, when the City was on Fire?

And is not the City on Fire now? Has not a devouring flame consumed Families innumerable? Are there not more Gentlemen and Tradesmen, Widows and Orphans ruin'd and reduc'd now by this cursed Conflagration, kindled by Bubbles and Directors? I say, are there not more of them than all the *Gaols* in *England* are able to hold? And shall these have no Shelter? (*Applebee*, 29 April 1721)

This striking picture of shelterless orphans makes an apt commentary on the poor families described in the *Journal*: similarly, the protest against confining debtors at such a moment echoes the feelings of H.F. against the policy of looking up infected persons in their house. It may be added that this paper of 29 April contains a reference to the avoidance of arrests during the Great Plague.

Many other examples could be given from the press during late 1720 and 1721. More than once we read of 'the Bubble Plague' (*Applebee*, 25 November 1721), or words to that effect. Even if Defoe himself had not been responsible for a single syllable of all this, it would indicate a general readiness to view the South Sea episode as a calamity on a par with the Plague of fifty-five years earlier. It would show how easily writers in the public press slipped into locutions which identified the two events, above all in their effects upon urban life. But of course this hypothesis is wildly unrealistic. It is certain that Defoe wrote some of the material I have quoted; highly likely that he wrote a considerable fraction of it; conceivable that he wrote every single word of it.

II

It has not, I think, been recognised up till now that Defoe wrote his account of the Great Plague with this looming connotation over his shoulder. The only glancing reference to the circumstances which I know occurs in a suggestive essay by W. Austin Flanders, which relates the *Journal* to 'modern urban experience'. The passage in Flanders's discussion is this:

Defoe's persistent concern with the economic consequences of the plague is fundamentally a concern with the consequences of urban capitalism. They are exactly those of an economic depression, a phenomenon which occurs in a capitalistic economy with as little apparent reason as disease itself. The fear of economic collapse, both personal and social, was ever-present to the minds of eighteenth-century businessmen and speculators. The collapse of the South-Sea Bubble in 1720—preceding the publication of the *Journal* by little over a year—provides a parallel to the plague and must have struck as much terror into the hearts of its victims as would the advent of a fatal disease. Defoe's images of the desolation of economic activity in London during the plague provides some of the *Journal's* most vivid moments.[10]

I shall not pursue all the political implications of this argument, and I will not point up the *personal* application of such insecurity to Defoe himself, with his chequered financial history. It is enough to say that Flanders detects a general congruence where I see something far more deeply interfused—a replay of the earlier historical process, enacted in a new sphere of life. For Defoe, South Sea constituted the second great national trauma in his lifetime. (Arguably the third, if we include the Great Fire of 1666: but his tone is always more cheerful in speaking of the Fire, which opened up opportunities: for modernisation, planning and better land-use, all things the land-speculator Defoe cared about.)[11] The Bubble was not a case of a random mishap in the capitalistic business cycle; rather, a political omen, a warning to the nation, a divine intervention, a glimpse of effects beyond more human causes. Its dimensions were theological, that is, as well as economic. With the indirection of genius, the artistic response Defoe hit upon was not a frontal account of the Bubble, but a narrative of its antecedent disaster. For the Plague was, in his mind, a typological equivalent for the new calamity.

Before turning directly to the text of the *Journal*, I wish to emphasise the lasting nature of this mental connection in Defoe's mind. The conjunction we have seen in several newspaper articles of 1720 and 1721 turns up in later works of that decade. Defoe goes on writing of the South Sea episode as a medical condition, as for instance in the first volume of his *Tour*:

> Pity and matter of Grief is it to think that Families, by Estate, able to appear in such a glorious Posture as this, should ever be Vulnerable by so mean a Disaster as that of Stock-Jobbing: But the *General*

Infatuation of the Day is a Plea for it; so that Men are not now blamed
on that Account: *South-Sea* was a general Possession; and if my Lord
Castlemain was Wounded by that Arrow shot in the Dark, 'twas a
Misfortune: But 'tis so much a Happiness, that it was not a mortal
Wound ...

   This cannot be said of some other Families in this County (Essex),
whose fine Parks and new-built Palaces are fallen under Forfeiture
and Alienations by the Misfortunes of the Times, and by the Ruin of
their Masters Fortunes in the *South-Sea* Deluge.[12]

Elsewhere in this work, Defoe speaks of the 'frantic' mood which
overtook England in 1720, 'when every Body's Heads were
turn'd with Projects and Stocks'.[13] He lingers over the 'General
Calamity of the late Directors' and the 'overthrow, and
Catastrophe of innumerable Wealthy City Families' who have
sunk under 'the Disasters of Trade'.[14] The vocabulary recalls *The
Complete English Tradesman*, where Defoe repeatedly cautions the
young businessman against 'Projects and Adventures' which
would only bring lead to bankruptcy and ruin. (See Chapter 8
above.) Everyone agrees that Defoe had a life-long concern with
the threat of financial disaster, with his own early misfortunes
continually present to his mind. What is interesting is the
developing tendency he shows in the 1720s to depict such disaster
in terms of bodily sickness or a total breakdown in mental and
physical health.

   When he does write about the plague in these later books, it is
commonly in terms of the economic collapse it brings in its wake.
Witness *A Plan of the English Commerce* (1728); Defoe there
mentions 'the late Accident of a Plague in *France*' as putting a
total stop to Franco-Spanish trade, and draws the familiar
conclusion:

   Should we ever see here such a fatal Time as that was in *France*, when
   Heaven sent the Infection among them at *Marseilles*, or as was here in
   1665, *God preserve us from it*, what a general Stop would it make to all
   our Trade? ... Yet this would not justly be call'd a Decay of our
   Commerce; it would indeed be a Wound, and a very desperate Blow
   to it for the Time; but as it was an Accident to the Trade, so the
   Cause being removed, the Trade would revive, return to its former
   Channel, and be the same as before.[15]

What we have here is two tenors for the same vehicle. The image is that of a wound or shock to the system; the state of the nation's health is affected by a sudden, although not necessarily irremediable, blow. In one case the debility is caused by the plague; in the other, it is occasioned by South Sea mania.

Other people used similar turns of phrase at this juncture of history. For example, when Parliament debated the initial attempts to restore credit after the bursting of the Bubble, the vehement Old Whig Lord Molesworth proclaimed that before 'remedies' were sought, it would be proper to seek out 'the cause and nature of the distemper'.[16] But Defoe is unusual on account of his sustained and near-compulsive recourse to such language. His well-established obsession with natural calamities provided a kind of reservoir of imagery, on which he could draw to describe the current threats to national life. Biblical cadences always came easily to Defoe, and it is his voice, surely, we hear when *Applebee* (19 November 1720) tells of the effects of the crash in Paris: 'These Things cause an universal Lamentation, and Multitudes of flourishing Families are utterly undone.' The same applies to the picture of a 'half-ruin'd City' which is given in a letter signed 'T. Sadler' (compare the occupation of H.F. in the *Journal*) on 22 October of that year. Here the writer deplores the 'Calamities of our Neighbours' and regrets that so little sympathy is being shown to those suffering under the great crash. 'No Age ever gave the like Instances of human Misery.'

One curious side-effect is reported on 28 January 1721:

We are assured, that the Number of Distemper'd Heads is so strangely encreas'd for some Months past, by the sudden rising and sudden falling of Men's Fortunes and Families, under the operation of South Sea Vomits, and other Bubble Physick; that there is not room to be had among the private BEDLAMS, *or Mad-Houses as they are call'd*, throughout the Town. And, that it is exceedingly difficult to get a Patient admitted, or to get Doctors of that kind to look after them, tho' several new ones are lately set up; and though some of those that were in Practice before have enlarg'd their Houses, and taken adjoyning Houses into their own, to make Conveniences for more Patients.

It is not clear whether the story may not be semi-facetious (as were many news items relating to Bubble 'lunacy'),[17] but the idea of a spreading infection, which would not be contained by the medical services available, has obvious links with the plague story. H.F. comments on the inadequate provision of pesthouses (74). The facts seemed almost to be playing into the hands of an observant writer. For anyone who could sense an imaginative connection between 1665 and 1720, the shocked and distracted condition of the nation sounded an increasing range of echoes. In my submission, it was Defoe who—consciously or unconsciously—first perceived the kind of tune which could be got from these reverberations.

III

The opening paragraph of the *Journal* refers to a number of rumours that plague had arisen on the Continent, especially Holland. However, its appearance in London is located in the death of two men 'said to be French-men' (1–2) in December 1664. There is a submerged parallel here, for the stock-jobbing mania was thought to have been imported from France, where John Law's Mississippi scheme provided a close analogue to South Sea. Indeed, the Bubble in its early stages was inflated partly by people arriving from Paris, who had speculated on the boom in the rue Quincampoix and had now turned their attentions to Exchange Alley. This urge to find an origin in foreign (particularly French) climes may be put down to simple xenophobia; but it is one of many tiny details in which the parallel holds with curious regularity.

The build-up of the infection in the spring is charted by an increase in mortality figures, reported in the weekly bills. Defoe begins to cite these almost at the very outset of his book, and it is in the wake of the rise in these statistics that popular 'uneasiness' grows. Similarly the approach of the financial disaster was heralded by the announcement of a more and more wildly inflated price of South Sea stock. There is of course a major difference: the climax of the Bubble would mean a sudden turn in the figures as the price plummeted downwards. But it is still true that the anxious observation of a rising tally attends both catastrophes: Defoe's account of the plague year follows the mortality figures with grim precision, and any narrative of the

Bubble must similarly focus on the steady and fatal rise in the price of stocks.

By May 1665 the outlook was growing more threatening (5-6); equally, the Bubble was filling up rapidly, with crowds of investors thronging the City. The lesser bubbles of more and more absurd projects began to mushroom; at the end of May and early June 1720 they had reached alarming numbers. Just as the City authorities had taken ineffective action to try and halt the plague, so Parliament passed a largely useless 'Bubble Act' at this juncture (with the royal assent on 9 June). Defoe tells us that 'from the first Week in *June*, the Infection spread in a dreadful Manner, and the Bills rose high' (6). Similarly, in 1720, hopes mounted and expectations soared: 'South Sea stock made its most sensational leap yet—from 610 to 870—in the first two days of June.'[18] The increasing ravages of the plague caused a good deal of public confusion: 'The Hurry of the People was such for some Weeks, that there was no getting at the Lord-Mayor's Door without exceeding Difficulty; there was such pressing and crouding there to get passes and Certificates of Health' (7). 1720 witnessed its own stampedes, but these were to get hold of the coveted shares; pick-pockets and vagrants mingled in the throng, and Jonathan Wild did a roaring business in restoring 'lost' property.[19] The King bestowed honours on the architects of the South Sea project, and a new development was to be laid out with the grand title of South Sea Square.

Into July both 'infections' went on their way. South Sea stock reached 1,000, briefly, and quotations remained above 900 for several weeks. The plague figures showed no tendency to level off, and in both cases the epicentre may be placed in July and August. South Sea reached its climax a little earlier: the slide had begun in the first and second weeks of September, whereas Defoe places the turn downwards in mortality figures in the week beginning 19 September (188-9). This refusal of history exactly to repeat itself is in some ways more apparent than real, for other figures quoted by H.F. show a definite turn-around at the start of September (205-6), exactly in parallel with the speculative mania.

As the two dramas unfold, several striking congruities emerge. There is the passing of the Bubble Act in June 1720, along with the order of the City Corporation to close up houses, published at 'the latter End of June' and operative from 1 July 1665. As Defoe notes, this order was in pursuance of an Act of Parliament, passed during an earlier plague emergency. Secondly, there is the terrible psychological effect witnessed on each occasion: suicides, distraction, 'Idiotism' (as H.F. puts it, 81), to set alongside the well-reported panic reactions to the collapse of the Bubble. Again, H.F. reports that 'the Court removed early, (*viz.*) in the Month of *June*' (15). In 1720 George I left for Hanover on 14 June, and was conveniently absent when the Bubble burst. He did, in fairness, return in November, whereas it was not until February 1666 that Charles II found it safe to return to Whitehall. It is also worth recalling that news of the Marseilles plague in August 1720 affected confidence in the market, and by mid-October the spread of the disease in France intensified public alarm when the Bubble was already properly burst. It was a further illustration of the way in which the two phenomena had strangely become interlinked. The plague was seen as a judgment on human greed, and people began to feel that 'the trade that had made men rich was being used by the Almighty to punish their ambition'. In October, such feelings 'deepened the depression' (John Carswell).[20] Again, plague and Bubble seem to have become common terms of a single metaphor.

Even the death scenes in the *Journal* have their strange analogues in the South Sea episode. One of the more harrowing cases described by H.F. is that of a mother whose nineteen-year-old daughter catches the disease and dies. The 'distracted' mother raves all over the house, and then within two or three weeks follows her daughter. H.F. comments on other cases where people were 'so frightened to die upon the Spot', and notes that the weekly bills even included '*frighted*' as a regular cause of death (56). The equivalent South Sea experience is described in *Applebee* for 15 October 1720, where a story concerning the perils of speculation is told by a correspondent signing himself 'Anti-Jobber'. The latter begins:

It would be ridiculous, at this Juncture, to write Letters to you, or give you the Trouble to print anything that did not relate to *South Sea Stock*: this is the only Theme of all the Pens that are now at Work.

The writer then turns to the case of a gentleman who had

received 'a sad Blow' from the stocks, and 'lay'd it so to Heart, that the Grief threw him into violent Passions and Convulsions, and carry'd him off. This last expression (to 'carry off') is of course an habitual form in plague narratives (see for instance *Journal*, 98). The gentleman in question had been elated by the prospect of a fortune and had sold his family estate to buy stock. Soon he was undone:

> I need not repeat to you the several degrees of Declination, by which this new Planet has sunk almost out of our Horizon; but our Gentleman,—seeing at last the utter Downfal, and that there was, in his Notion, no more Possibility of its rising again, then he thought there was before of its falling,—came back into the Country, and, in a Word, fall sick, and dy'd. Indeed, it was fear'd, he would have dy'd by no other Hands than his own; but Providence order'd that Part otherwise.

The story is made the occasion for a warning against the whole Bubble mania, delivered as a sermon by the parson of the parish in which the gentleman lived. However, I adduce the episode not for its theological bearings, but as a foreshadowing of the death by distraction in the *Journal*. South Sea fortunes, says Anti-Jobber, were 'founded in Fraud ... and lost by Distraction'.

The identification obviously will not hold in every single particular. History does not work like that. The clearest disparity resides in the fact that the events of 1665 represent an initial upward curve of disaster, intensifying through the summer, and alleviating around September. Those of 1720 represent a period of bemused elation as the price of stock rises, culminating in the heady optimism of midsummer, and then tumbling into disaster around September. The trajectories are equivalent in shape, but one is an inverted image of the other. Nevertheless, the similarities are at least as apparent, and more suggestive. For anyone taking up the theme of civic breakdown in the wake of a major disaster, it involved little stretching of the facts to see 1665 as an analogue of 1720—or vice versa.

I do not claim that Defoe was 'really' writing about the South Sea episode when he composed the *Journal*. My contention is that some of the deeper imaginative currents of the book must have been set in motion by his recent experience in witnessing—and chronicling for the press—the traumas of the Bubble year. This is not like saying that *La Peste* is beneath the surface a study of the Nazi concentration camps: I am postulating an imaginative transfer of a quasi-literal, rather than a symbolic, kind. When H.F. writes of the deserted city, the 'desolating of some of the Streets' (17) and the closed buildings, he is echoing many contemporary descriptions of London after the Bubble: 'this half-ruin'd City', as T. Sadler termed it. When the *Journal* alludes to the 'desperate' acts of people during the plague (55), we are close to the picture of the 'frighted' South Sea faces painted by the Leicestershire grazier. In each case we have the gradual onset of a seemingly unstoppable contagion, with unavailing attempts by those in authority to quell the outbreak. To those sharing in the South Sea euphoria, the rise in stocks was a very different thing from the catalogue of plague disasters: but to Defoe, who had much earlier detected the villainy of stock-jobbers and anatomised Exchange Alley in unfriendly terms, the process would have seemed not at all remote. For, if my findings have any validity, then the *Journal* must operate as a damning indictment of the South Sea scheme: the parallel can work no other way.

It would have been impossible for anyone to write on the theme of national disaster in 1721 (when composition of the *Journal* was almost certainly under way) without an awareness, at some level, of contemporary history. Least of all could Defoe have done this, when week by week during that year—as in its predecessor—he was penning items for the press on the 'Calamity', the Bubble. (Many of the items took a fictional form, moreover.)[21] There is considerable evidence to show that the drama of 1720 remained deeply etched on Defoe's consciousness for the rest of his life. We have seen how often plague and South Sea crash meshed into one another in people's minds and in their language. Is it plausible, then, to assume that Defoe could have written the *Journal* without sensing any of the parallels I have indicated? And even if, with extreme caution, we stop short of attributing any degree of conscious perception on his part, does that nullify the resonances we can discern in the text of the *Journal?*

A literal-minded answer would be that the book never mentions South-Sea; granted an adult witness as first-person narrator, that was unavoidable. A more responsive account, alive to the characteristic process by which Defoe moved from fact to fiction, might reveal the *Journal* as an even richer book than we thought it. Propaganda for the government's quarantine measures, to offset plague, certainly; but also propaganda in favour of Walpole's attemptes at financial reconstruction, by way of a plea not to repeat the follies of the Bubble. Defoe did care about public health, and he was deeply interested in natural disasters: but he had, too, a long-standing preoccupation with such things as national credit, financial probity, and the means by which an embarrassed trader could climb back to respectability and affluence.[22] In this light, the (broadly) happy ending of the *Journal* may be seen as a wish-fulfilment: a hope that England may overcome the disasters of 1720, through wise government and cooperation on the part of people[23]—much as the threat of the plague had finally been averted. The *Journal* ends with a passage drawing attention to the complacent ease with which most men and women shrugged off the events of 1665. The fear that this should be repeated, in the case of the shocks only recently experienced in 1720, is a hidden theme of 'the Account of this calamitous Year' (248): a submerged anxiety in this masterly study of a community *in extremis*.

Notes

1. Defoe's involvement in journalism at this date was first fully revealed by William Lee, *Daniel Defoe: His Life and Recently Discovered Writings* (London, 1869; rptd Hildersheim, 1968). Subsequent research has tended to substantiate Lee's attributions, and I follow his text for quotations. Page references are not normally supplied where I record a date, as Lee prints items in chronological order; all citations here are from Vol. II of Lee's work. Items from *Applebee* dealing with the plague are also available in *Selected Poetry and Prose of Daniel Defoe*, ed. Michael F. Shugrue (New York, 1968), pp. 204-14.

2. Lee, II, pp. 283-4.

3. Quoted by Carswell, p. 194. The main lines of my account of the Bubble are drawn from this work.

4. For an account of these measures, and opposition within the trading community, see A.J. Henderson, *London and the National Government* (Durham, N.C., 1945), pp. 33-45, 49, 52-3. Henderson notes Defoe's share in the publicity campaign on behalf of the government, pp. 44-5.

5. For example, in *The Anatomy of Exchange Alley* (1719), Defoe had set out a whole series of political evils which would result from allowing the stock-jobbers too much power: 'For when statesmen turn jobbers the state may be jobbed' (*The Versatile Defoe*, ed. Laura Ann Curtis (London, 1979), p. 273).
6. *A Journal of the Plague Year*, ed. Louis A. Landa (London, 1969), pp. xiii, xv. All references are to this edition: page references are supplied in the text, within parentheses.
7. *Journal of the Plague Year*, ed. Landa, pp. xv-xvii.
8. For other examples see Lee, II, 298, 325. A parodic version of South Sea suicides appeared in *Applebee*, 14 January 1721.
9. See Defoe, *Tour*, I, 169.
10. W. Austin Flanders, 'Defoe's *Journal of the Plague Year* and the modern urban experience', *Centennial Review*, XVI (1972), 328-48; rptd in *Daniel Defoe: A Collection of Critical Essays*, ed. Max Byrd (Englewood Cliffs, N.J., 1976), pp. 150-69 (quotation from pp. 159-60). See also Byrd's book *London Transformed: Images of the City in the Eighteenth Century* (New Haven, 1978), pp. 30-43.
11. For this aspect of Defoe, see Spiro Peterson, 'Defoe and Westminster, 1696-1706', *ECS* XII (1979), 306-38.
12. Defoe, *Tour*, I, 90-1. See also p. 144 above.
13. Defoe *Tour*, I, 160. Defoe's expression here is 'one unhappy *Stock Jobbing Year*', which chimes with his phrasing at the end of the *Journal*.
14. Defoe *Tour*, I, 159, 169.
15. *A Plan of the English Commerce* (Oxford, 1928), pp. 194-5.
16. Quoted by Virginia Cowles, *The Great Swindle* (London, 1960), p. 154. Similarly, Bishop Atterbury spoke in the Lords and compared the South Sea Company to the plague then raging in France: see G.V. Bennett, *The Tory Crisis in Church and State 1688-1730* (Oxford, 1975), p. 226.
17. It is impossible to check the suggestion that the number of madhouses had increased in the wake of the Bubble, as 'officially documented information about the number of private madhouses, their capacity, distribution and proprietors, is not available prior to 1774': William Ll. Parry-Jones, *The Trade in Lunacy* (London, 1972), p. 29. For South Sea investors as 'lunatics', see Pope to Atterbury, 23 September 1720: Pope *Corr*, II, 54.
18. Carswell, pp. 156-7.
19. Looting and petty crime is described as going on during the plague: *Journal* p. 15.
20. Carswell, p. 200.
21. See for example Lee, II, pp. 282-4, 286-7, 292-3, 302-5, 316-19, 323-5, 327-30, 333-6, and *passim*: mostly involving an imaginary correspondent, but some relating fictional narratives also.
22. See Peter Earle, *The World of Defoe* (London, 1976), pp. 239-41, 336 n. 51, for a helpful summary of Defoe's attitude towards financial collapse.
23. See for example Lee, II, 319-22. Several papers seek to arouse resentment against the 'Chief Agents of the Nation's Misfortunes ... the Grand Confederates in the whole *South Sea* Disaster' (Lee, II, 436).

AFTERWORD

A recurrent theme in the critical endeavour underlying these studies has been the location of a particular occasion or starting-point for major texts of the 1720s. I should be reluctant to claim that such things can ever explain a work, in the sense of providing a single and definitive way of reading the text. But the historical spur to action may pervade the author's imagination long after his work has expanded, rhetorically and thematically, to embrace issues very remote from that original impulse. In Chapter 2 I sought to demonstrate that Swift's 'Southern Journey' had more links with the Bubble phenomenon and the whole mania for projecting than has been realised until now. At the same time we must hold on to the recognition that Gulliver's adventures expand beyond the temporal into metaphysical and moral regions which are of permanent interest. Similarly I argue in Chapter 9 that Defoe's *Tour* blends close observation of recent changes in the nation with a larger awareness of the cycle of growth and decay: and in Chapter 5 that Pope's *Court Ballad* has a precise occasion in mind beneath the general air of easy-going satire on court life. It is in the rediscovery of such 'external' promptings that several of the essays centre: together with the attempt to show how these concerns are internalised, through the medium of structure, linguistic texture or some other literary agency.

I hope that some kind of family resemblance will have emerged between the different works studied. Remote as their authors sometimes were in outlook, there apprehension of what was significant in contemporary history tended to merge in a surprising way. All four writers considered wrote, directly or indirectly, about the Jacobite rising, the Bubble, and Jonathan Wild. Their compositions trace an important line of thought based first upon the coming of the Hanoverians, and second upon the dominance of Walpole. Their literary procedures vary in character and in tone: but the world they inhabit has a marked individuality, running across the surface differences in style of theme. Whatever their intellectual interests or classical antecedents may have been, they lived very much in the present. Their encounter with their own age was full-bodied and immediate—this is true of Pope as well as of Defoe. It is a disservice to men of this stamp if we bury their satire beneath the veils of rhetoric, or deflect their vital commitment with the reflectors and refractors of irony. Our task as readers is, instead, to reconstruct and not to deconstruct the text: to fight out our understandings, so to speak, in the dust and the heat of the age. It may not sound a very ambitious undertaking, when put alongside the more grandiose pretensions of literary theory: but it may still be the most rewarding kind of encounter with the past which is open to us.

INDEX